The Complete
CARE PLAN
MANUAL
for Long-Term Care
REVISED EDITION

Connie S. March

AHA American Hospital Publishing, Inc.
An American Hospital Association Company
Chicago

Library of Congress Cataloging-in-Publication Data

March, Connie S.
    The complete care plan manual for long-term care / Connie S. March. – Rev. ed.
        p.   cm.
    Includes index.
    ISBN 1-55648-184-5
    1. Long-term care of the sick–Handbooks, manuals, etc.
2. Nursing care plans–Handbooks, manuals, etc. 3. Nursing home care–Handbooks, manuals, etc. I. Title.
    [DNLM: 1. Long-Term Care–handbooks. 2. Nursing Homes–United States–handbooks. 3. Homes for the Aged–United States–handbooks. 4. Patient Care Planning–handbooks. WX 39 M315ca 1997]
RT120.L64M38 1997
362. 1'6–dc21
DNLM/DLC
for Library of Congress   96-40182
                                                                          CIP

Catalog no. 130106

© copyright 1997 by Connie S. March.

Published by American Hospital Publishing, Inc.,
an American Hospital Association company

Printed in the USA

AHA is a service mark of the American Hospital Association used under license by American Hospital Publishing, Inc.

Marsha Mildred, Senior Editor
Nancy Charpentier, Editor
Peggy DuMais, Assistant Production Manager
Marcia Bottoms, Director, Books Division
Lucy Lesiak, Cover Designer

American Hospital Publishing, Inc.
737 North Michigan Avenue
Chicago, IL 60611

Contents

About the Author v

Acknowledgments vi

Introduction vii

   Components of a Useful Care Plan viii

   Using This Care Plan Manual xi

   Case Study and Sample Care Plan xvi

1. Delirium 1

2. Cognitive Loss/Dementia 7

3. Visual Function 11

4. Communication 15

5. ADL Functional/Rehabilitation Potential 19

   Mobility 19

   Dressing 24

   Eating 27

   Toileting 29

   Personal Hygiene 31

   Bathing 33

6. Urinary Incontinence and Indwelling Catheter 35

7. Psychosocial Well-Being 39

8. Mood State 47

Contents

9. Behavior Problems 53

10. Activities 59

11. Falls 63

12. Nutritional Status 65

13. Feeding Tubes 71

14. Dehydration/Fluid Maintenance 75

15. Dental Care 79

16. Pressure Ulcers 83

17. Psychotropic Drug Use 87

18. Physical Restraints 91

Appendix. NANDA-Approved Nursing Diagnoses 95

About the Author

Connie S. March is president of Cor Unum, the elder care holding company of ServantCor in Kankakee, Illinois. In this position, she provides administrative leadership for nursing homes and other eldercare services within the ServantCor system. She has worked in the area of geriatrics since 1978. Her experience ranges from teaching introductory courses in geriatric health care to nursing and medical students to providing primary health care to nursing home residents in conjunction with physicians. Ms. March has been active in various health care organizations, including Life Services Network board and committees; Catholic Health Association Board and committees; Catholic Conference of Illinois, Homes for the Aging Division Advisory Board; and Illinois Department on Aging Alzheimer's Disease Task Force. She has written on a number of elder care issues. Ms. March received her bachelor's and master's degrees in nursing from the University of Illinois College of Nursing.

Acknowledgments

I would like to thank everyone for their contributions toward this project, especially the following:

- Champaign County Nursing Home, for initiating the original project.
- ServantCor, for an environment conducive to creative productivity. Special thanks go to Joe Feth, ServantCor CEO, for his encouragement and support.

- Book reviewers, who provided invaluable feedback used to revise this edition of the care plan manual.
- Larry and Ben, for their patience and understanding during the many hours away from them while I revised this manual.

I could not have done it without each and every one of you.

Introduction

If you were to ask nurses and other health care professionals to list the three greatest changes in the past 10 years in providing care for long-term care residents, one change they would all include is the increased amount of paperwork that is required to document care. In itself, the documentation of resident planning and care serves a number of positive functions. It provides a channel of communication between caregivers from different shifts and between caregivers from different disciplines. Over time, documentation is a record of a resident's progress or lack of progress. Documentation provides a means for measuring quality of care.

Although all of these are important justifications for the time health care professionals spend in documentation, often the overriding reason is that licensure and certification agencies require it. Specific requirements may differ from state to state, but an appropriate care plan for each resident that is measurable, reviewed regularly, and developed by a multidisciplinary team is a nationally accepted component of high-quality long-term or nursing home care. Documentation of the reimbursable aspects of care identified on care plans is used by some governmental agencies as a means of determining reimbursement for residents' care. It is evident that requirements in this area will become more stringent in the future. The documentation of the reimbursable aspects of care should not be confused with the documentation of the quality of care called for by regulatory and accrediting bodies.

The purpose of this manual is to give long-term care providers a flexible, easy-to-use tool for developing resident care plans that maximize the use of staff time, ensure the quality of individualized care, and meet regulatory requirements. We hope that you will make it a practical tool by adapting it to meet the needs of your residents and staff. The rest of this section describes the components of a care plan and provides guidelines for using this care plan manual.

Components of a Useful Care Plan

This manual's approach is called *useful* or *functional care planning*. From the perspective of the long-term care staff, this approach is practical. It uses simple, descriptive words that can be understood by all, and it is geared to use by multidisciplinary teams. From the resident's perspective, it focuses on the functions required for everyday living: eating, moving, grooming, bathing, dressing, toileting, and so on. It also focuses on critical clinical conditions commonly observed in long-term care residents.

The care plan should outline the resident's most *crucial* problems. Attempting to work on too many problems at the same time can overwhelm and confuse the staff. Although there is no magic number, ordinarily only about five or six problem areas can be addressed effectively for each resident.

Care planning involves four steps: (1) assessment, (2) planning, (3) implementation, and (4) evaluation and reassessment.

Assessment

The assessment identifies the resident's strengths and weaknesses and is the first step in the care planning process. To make the assessment, staff members from all disciplines involved with the resident provide information. The Omnibus Budget Reconciliation Act (OBRA) of 1987 mandated use of the minimum data set (MDS) to assess all residents in nursing homes certified by Medicare or Medicaid. The MDS provides a consistent format for assessment. This assessment has been revised into a version known as MDS 2.0. Potential problem areas are triggered. Triggers for each condition refer to problems, risks of developing a problem, or rehabilitation potential. Triggered conditions require additional assessment utilizing specific guidelines identified by the Health Care Financing Administration's Resident Assessment Protocols (RAPs). Use of the MDS and RAPs is described in various publications, such as the *Resident Assessment Instrument Training Manual and Resource Guide*.[1] Because of the availability of resource material for these areas, completing the MDS and RAPs is not discussed in this manual. Rather, the focus is on producing useful individualized care plans *after* the resident has been assessed by using the MDS and appropriate RAPs. Analysis of information leads to the second step in the process, planning.

Planning

Planning consists of three tasks: formulating problem/need statements, developing measurable goals, and planning interventions, with delegation of each intervention to a responsible discipline.

Problem/need statements may refer to anything of concern to the resident or to a lack of something useful to, required by, or desired by the resident. The statement is composed of three distinct parts (see table 1):

1. Stem statement
   - Identifies area of the resident's life in which a problem or need exists
   - States problem as a noun
   Example: constipation
2. Connector
   - Connects problem or need with the causative or contributing factors (etiologies)
   - Uses words "related to" or "associated with"
   Example: related to
3. Etiology (causative or contributing factor[s])
   - Identifies the cause(s) or contributing factor(s) of the problem/need
   - States cause or contributing factor as a noun
   - Names no more than two causes or contributing factors for each problem/need
   Example: low oral fluid intake

Example of problem statement: Constipation related to low oral fluid intake

Throughout the manual, the problems/needs are cross-referenced with the nursing diagnoses as approved by the North American Nursing Diagnosis Association (NANDA) at its eleventh conference in 1994. The cross referencing is not intended to be all-inclusive. The appendix provides a complete listing of nursing diagnoses approved at that conference.

Residents may be at risk of developing certain problems, and these potential problems may also be stated on the care plan. *Example:* Potential for skin breakdown over coccyx related to urinary incontinence.

Staff members must consider several points when formulating problem/need statements. Problems should be resident centered rather than staff centered. Problems or causes should not be stated purely as medical diagnoses, treatable only by the physician; instead, they should be treatable by members of the multidisciplinary team who are in the nursing home frequently. Problems should be written in simple terms and should be stated as specifically and clearly as possible.

The stem of the problem statement leads to the formulation of the *goal*. The goal should state, in measurable

Table 1.   Problem/Need Statement

Stem Statement (brief statement of resident's problem)	Connector ("related to" or "associated with")	Etiology (Cause that can be treated by multidisciplinary team)
Constipation	Related to	Low oral fluid intake
Relates to resident's goal		Relates to interventions
Example: Will have bowel movement every three days.		*Example:* Identify preferred liquids.
		Give fluids orally with following schedule: 500 cc—11 p.m. to 7 a.m. 1000 cc—7 a.m. to 3 p.m. 1000 cc—3 p.m. to 11 p.m.
		Record intake and output.
		Record bowel movements (related to problem rather than to cause but needed for assessment and evaluation).

Source: Adapted from Veterans' Administration Medical Center, Danville, IL.

behavioral terms, what the resident is expected to accomplish. To help ensure that the goal is resident centered, it should begin: "The resident will . . ." or "Mrs. Brown will . . . ." *Example:* The resident will have a bowel movement at least every three days.

A goal has four components:

1. Resident identifier
   * Identifies who is to accomplish goal
   * Is stated as noun—may be general or specific
   Example: The resident (general) or Mrs. Brown (specific)
2. Resident action or behavior
   * Specifies activity to be accomplished by resident
   * Must be observable
   * Must be measurable
   * Must be realistic
   * Is generally stated as action verb
   Example: will walk
3. Performance criteria
   * Specify amount or type of behavior or action needed to accomplish goal
   Example: 50 feet
4. Qualifying conditions
   * Specify modifiers or assistance allowed resident in meeting goal
   Example: with a rolling walker

Example of goal statement: Mrs. Brown will walk 50 feet with a rolling walker.

Measurable goals for the resident may be incremental. Although a long-range goal may be identified, a series of short-range goals must be met before achieving the long-range goal. State the first goal to be reached as the initial goal for the problem. After the first goal, state the next goal. Caregivers should proceed down the list of short-range goals until the original long-range goal becomes the goal named on the care plan. For example:

Problem	Goals
6/10/97—Stage-4 purulent draining decubitus ulcer on coccyx (4 cm × 3 cm × 5 cm deep) related to urinary incontinence and inability to change position independently	The resident will: 1. Have no drainage from decubitus on coccyx by 6/24/97. 2. Have a reduction in size of decubitus to 3 cm × 2 cm × 4 cm by 7/10/97. 3. Have reduction in size of decubitus to 2 cm × 1 cm × 2 cm by 8/1/97. 4. Have reduction in size of decubitus to 1 cm × 0.5 cm × 1 cm by 8/22/97. 5. Have healed decubitus by 10/1/97.

Components of a Useful Care Plan

Although the healing of the ulcer was the ultimate goal in the preceding example, incremental goals had to be met before the long-range goal could be achieved. In this example, teamwork between resident and staff was necessary to accomplish the goals. Achieving the long-range goal does *not* depend entirely on the staff, and thus the goal maintains a resident-centered focus.

Planning interventions is the next task after the assessment is completed and problem statements and goals are established. The interventions delineate the activities that various members of the multidisciplinary team, the resident, or significant others can take to assist the resident in meeting the goal. In general, many interventions may be required or desired for each problem. The statement of each intervention should start with a verb. Interventions are partially dependent on the strengths of each individual resident. Therefore, interventions will often vary for different residents who have identical problems and goals.

Writing interventions tends to be the easiest part of the care plan for the staff. Staff members must remember, however, that each outlined intervention should be useful in meeting the specific goal. Miscellaneous interventions should not be added to a care plan, because they will dilute the effectiveness of the planned interventions. (*Example:* Care must be given to skin around a colostomy stoma. Note, however, that this care should not be added as an intervention to an unrelated problem solely because it has to be recorded somewhere.) Kardexes® or assignment sheets can list miscellaneous tasks not addressed in the care plan.

Implementation

Implementing the care plan is the third step of the care planning process. Implementation should be carried out as listed on the care plan. The timing, repetitions, and sequencing should be followed precisely. Responsible persons or departments are designated on the care plan to ensure consistency of implementation.

Evaluation and Reassessment

Evaluating outcomes and reassessing the resident to determine whether the goal has been met is the fourth step. If the goal has not been accomplished, the following questions should be asked:

- Was the goal realistic?
- Was the goal stated in measurable terms?
- Did the interventions help the resident achieve the goal?
- Was the time frame realistic?
- Were the interventions realistic?
- Were the interventions carried out as stated?
- Were the appropriate disciplines or caregivers identified for each intervention?
- Was this really a problem for this resident?

Answers to these questions should identify deficiencies in the plan and direct staff in correcting those deficiencies.

One final warning: The simplest terminology possible should be used in writing care plans to ensure that all members of the team understand the plan. A beautifully written plan that is understood by only one or two people on the team has limited value.

Using This Care Plan Manual

This manual is designed to simplify the task of developing problem/need statements, goals, and interventions in the long-term care setting. It is divided into 23 areas and is set up to move staff through the steps outlined in the preceding section.

The following is a step-by-step guide for using this manual:

1. *Conduct a complete holistic assessment of resident.* The multidisciplinary team performs a holistic assessment that considers the resident's strengths. At minimum, assessment should include completion of the Minimum Data Set 2.0, which addresses physiological, psychological, social, self-care (activities of daily living), and financial areas. The spiritual component may be assessed separately or incorporated into an assessment tool that goes beyond the MDS 2.0.

2. *Identify problems or needs and etiologies.* Problems or needs are specific statements that list anything that causes concern to the resident or that identify a lack of something useful to, required by, or desired by the resident. Completion of appropriate RAPs will assist in identifying problems to be included in the care plan.
   a. Identify the general problem area.
   b. Turn to the index of the manual.
   c. Find the page numbers for the general area identified (for example, "eating, problems with," p. 27–28).
   d. Turn to the pages identified.
   e. Scan the problems/needs list.
   f. Pick out the problem/need of the resident.
   g. Turn to the etiologies page of the pertinent section.
   h. Scan the etiologies.
   i. Pick out etiologies or factors causing or contributing to the problem/need for the resident.
   j. On the care plan form (figure 1), enter the date the problem was listed. Also write in the problem/need statement, the connecting words "related to" or "associated with," and the etiologies identified for the resident.
   Example: 6/10/97 Inability to chew food properly related to improperly fitting dentures.

3. *Identify measurable goals.* Goals should address the desired outcome of treatment, medications, procedures, and interventions used to combat a problem.
   a. Turn to the goals list in the same section used for problems/needs and etiologies.
   b. Scan the list of sample goals.

c. Identify the goal appropriate for the resident.
   d. Conclude the statement with the date targeted for goal achievement. This date identifies when goal achievement will be formally evaluated.
   e. On the care plan form, insert the goal statement and target date in the *Goal* column.
   Example: The resident will be able to chew food properly by 6/30/97.

4. *Identify interventions.* Interventions that will assist in problem resolution and goal achievement are identified. Interventions generally relate to etiology but also may relate to the problem/need statement.
   a. Turn to the interventions list in the pertinent section of the manual.
   b. Scan the list of possible interventions given.
   c. Identify all interventions that may be used in problem resolution and goal achievement.
   d. On the care plan form, describe identified interventions. Make interventions specific for goal achievement for the resident.
   e. Add any interventions that are appropriate for the resident but are not listed in the catalog.
   Examples: (1) Refer to dentist for evaluation and recommendations. (2) Give food that is easily chewed and swallowed by resident. (3) Remain with resident during meals.

5. *Identify responsible discipline.* Discipline(s) directly responsible for monitoring and assisting the resident with each intervention should be specified.
   a. Decide which discipline(s) will be responsible for each intervention.
   b. On the care plan form, list the responsible discipline(s) in the *Responsible Party* column next to each intervention.
   Example: (1) Head nurse, (2) dietitian, (3) nursing assistants.

6. *Implement plan.* Responsible parties complete care as outlined on the care plan.

7. *Evaluate care plan.* The care plan is evaluated when the target dates have been reached or at any time that is indicated by a change in the resident's condition or circumstances.
   a. Use a colored marker to highlight resolved problems, achieved goals, and achieved interventions, along with the responsible discipline.
   b. Place the date of goal achievement in *Date Goal Achieved/Comments* column of the care plan form.
   c. Place comments regarding the plan in the *Comments* column.

Using This Care Plan Manual

Figure 1. Care Plan Form

NAME _____ FLOOR _____ ROOM _____ LEVEL OF CARE _____ Page _____

PHYSICIAN _____ DIAGNOSES _____

DATE	PROBLEM/NEED	GOAL TARGET DATE	INTERVENTIONS	RESPONSIBLE PARTY	DATE GOAL ACHIEVED/ COMMENTS

Example: 6/25/97 Goal achieved. Dentures relined. Eating all of regular diet.

d. If a goal is not achieved by the target date, examine why the goal was not met.

e. Adjust the area found to be at fault. This may mean restating the goal, adjusting the target date, adjusting interventions, being faithful to the outlined interventions, or delegating interventions to different disciplines.

f. Draw a line in ink through problems that have not been resolved but are being deleted from the active care plan. This allows immediate differentiation between resolved problems (highlighted with colored marker) and unresolved problems taken off active care plan (crossed out in ink). Also cross out any outdated or inappropriate information.

One problem/need should be placed on each care plan page to allow for the addition of new goal statements and/or new interventions. This avoids the need to rewrite care plans with each revision.

This care plan manual is intended only as a guide in planning care for residents. It should stimulate you to think of problems, goals, and interventions appropriate for your residents that may not be listed and to adapt listed problems, goals, and interventions to precisely suit specific residents or situations.

Two forms are included in this manual as adjuncts to the basic care plan form. A care plan worksheet should be completed for each resident before the care plan conference (figure 2). Staff members from all disciplines are encouraged to list any problems or strengths that they identify in the resident. There is no right or wrong wording; the purpose of the worksheet is communication. The care plan worksheet can be a useful device in formulating the care plan. It can be discarded after the conference or retained as a continuous feedback mechanism.

A care plan fact sheet should be used for each resident (figure 3). It contains identifying information about each resident, as well as the signatures of all persons who have participated in the care plan formulation and review. Care plans should be reviewed after any significant change in the resident's condition or at least every three months.

This manual is designed for use in long-term care facilities. The manual is flexible enough, however, that it can be used, with some adaptation, in any long-term care situation, such as adult day-care centers, case management systems, and home health services. It is also possible to use the manual effectively in acute care settings with elderly patients.

Using This Care Plan Manual

Figure 2. Care Plan Worksheet

NAME _____ FLOOR _____ ROOM _____			
DATE	PROBLEMS	STRENGTHS	DATE

Figure 3. *Care Plan Fact Sheet*

NAME _____ FLOOR _____ ROOM _____

DATE OF BIRTH _____ PHYSICIAN _____

DIAGNOSES _____

_____

_____

CARE PLAN CONFERENCE DATE _____
CARE PLAN PARTICIPANTS

_____   _____

_____   _____

_____   _____

_____   _____

CARE PLAN REVIEW DATE 1 _____
CARE PLAN PARTICIPANTS

_____   _____

_____   _____

_____   _____

_____   _____

CARE PLAN REVIEW DATE 2 _____
CARE PLAN PARTICIPANTS

_____   _____

_____   _____

_____   _____

_____   _____

Case Study and Sample Care Plan

The best way to demonstrate the use of the care planning process is through an actual example. A sample care plan has been worked out for Mrs. Brown, who is a typical resident of a skilled nursing facility. The sample plan is illustrated in figure 4.

Mrs. Brown is a 78-year-old woman who resides in a skilled nursing facility. She has a husband, who visits her daily, and three daughters, who live out of town. Two daughters live out of state; the third lives 30 miles from the nursing home and visits her mother weekly. One of the daughters from out of state visits yearly and demands that her mother's care change drastically in terms of scheduling and intensity. This daughter has no health care background and has difficulty accepting the decline in her mother's condition.

Mrs. Brown has had Parkinson's disease for 25 years. Her husband has taken her all over the world for treatment. She has had a *ventricular shunt*, which has not helped. Currently she is taking Sinemet® by prescription. Her physician visits every month and would visit more frequently if requested. Mrs. Brown has been diagnosed as also having Alzheimer's disease. No workup was performed before this diagnosis was made.

Mrs. Brown has become progressively debilitated over the past three years. She bears almost no weight when transferring. She was ambulated daily by the staff until she was being dragged rather than walked down the hall because of her weight bearing, rigidity, and balance problems. Mrs. Brown spends most of the day in a geriatric chair. She is positioned with a posey vest but still leans markedly forward or to either side. Self-feeding is difficult because of her leaning forward into the tray, poor strength in her arms and hands, rigidity, and fatigue.

Mrs. Brown does not respond when her husband attempts to communicate with her. She does open her eyes, smile, and speak softly when her favorite nurse talks to her. Fatigue prevents any interaction over one or two minutes long. Mrs. Brown loves puppies, music, fashionable clothes, and children. Her former occupation was teaching high-school science.

Case Study Sample Care Plan: Mrs. Brown

1. Eating was identified as a problem area.
2. Turn to the index and look for the appropriate category, *eating.*
3. Turn to p. 27. Scan the problems/needs list. Identify "Does not convey food into mouth."
4. List the date that the problem was placed on the care plan in the *Date* column of the care plan form.
5. Write "Resident does not convey food into mouth" in the *Problem/Need* column.
6. Scan the etiologies list for possible causative factors for the resident not conveying food to mouth. "Impaired arm strength" is identified. "Consistent leaning position" is also an etiology but is not listed.
7. Write the connecting phrase "related to" and "impaired arm strength and consistent leaning position" in the *Problem/Need* column. The problem reads: "Resident does not convey food into mouth related to impaired arm strength and consistent leaning position."
8. Look at the goal statements listed. Identify a statement that is appropriate for this situation: "The resident will convey food to own mouth by _____."
9. Write the goal and the target date for reaching the goal in the *Goal* column.
10. Turn to p. 28. Read through all the suggested interventions. On the care plan form, write down all interventions that are appropriate for this situation. Add to the care plan any intervention that is appropriate but is not listed.
11. Identify the responsible party for each intervention in the *Responsible Party* column on the care plan form.

Page numbers are given for each component of the remaining problems on the sample care plan (figure 4). This allows you to follow the process outlined above for each problem and further familiarize yourself with the process.

One of Mrs. Brown's daughters was identified as having a problem. This problem was addressed on the resident's care plan (see figure 4). Placing family problems that must be addressed by staff members on the care plan is optional, but the resident is affected whenever a family member has a significant problem related to the resident's care.

More than one problem is listed on each page of the sample care plan because of space considerations. However, when formulating plans for residents, it is recommended that only one problem be addressed on each page to allow for future revisions without rewriting the entire plan.

Remember, this care plan manual is intended only as a guide. Not all possible problems/needs, goals, and interventions for every situation are listed. Formulate and list components in any of these areas that are appropriate for your residents but are not listed in this manual. Also, adapt any phrase or statement as needed to precisely fit any given situation.

Figure 4. Sample Care Plan

NAME _Mrs. Brown_   FLOOR _2 East_   ROOM _21-A_   LEVEL OF CARE _Skilled_   Page _1_

PHYSICIAN _Dr. Smith_   DIAGNOSES _Parkinson's disease, Alzheimer's disease_

DATE	PROBLEM/NEED	GOAL TARGET DATE	INTERVENTIONS	RESPONSIBLE PARTY	DATE GOAL ACHIEVED/ COMMENTS
6/10/97	Resident does not convey food to mouth related to impaired arm strength and consistent leaning position (p. 27)	Resident will convey food to own mouth by 9/10/97 (p. 27)	1. Offer small feedings five times a day 2. Position upright for meals 3. Allow resident extra time to eat (p. 28) 4. Assist resident to eat after resident becomes fatigued (p. 28) 5. Remain near resident during meals (p. 28) 6. Refer to OT for evaluation and recommendations (p. 28)	Dietary Nursing Dietary, nursing Nursing Nursing Occupational therapy	
6/10/97	Daughter experiencing severe stress related to resident's level of functioning (p. 40)	Daughter will state she is experiencing a decrease in stress level by 9/10/97	1. Give support to daughter regarding resident's level of functioning 2. Provide information to daughter regarding any change in resident's condition 3. Allow daughter to air feelings regarding resident's condition, care, and prognosis 4. Introduce daughter to staff caring for resident 5. Provide consistent caregivers to resident when possible 6. Review care plan with daughter when possible	Social work, nursing Social work, nursing Social work, administration Nursing Nursing Social work, nursing	

(Continued on next page)

Case Study and Sample Care Plan

Figure 4. (Continued)

NAME _Mrs. Brown_____ FLOOR _2 East___ ROOM _21-A____ LEVEL OF CARE _Skilled___ Page _2_____

PHYSICIAN _Dr. Smith_____ DIAGNOSES _Parkinson's disease, Alzheimer's disease_____

DATE	PROBLEM/NEED	GOAL TARGET DATE	INTERVENTIONS	RESPONSIBLE PARTY	DATE GOAL ACHIEVED/ COMMENTS
6/10/97	Impaired mobility related to loss of position sense and decreased strength in lower extremities (p. 19)	Resident will move about in bed without assistance by 9/10/97 (p. 21)	1. Refer to physical therapy for evaluation and recommendations (p. 22) 2. Have resident attempt all movements by self before offering assistance (p. 22) 3. Provide alternating periods of rest and activity (p. 23) 4. Give verbal cues to resident regarding each movement required a. systematically b. singly (p. 22)	Physical therapy Nursing Nursing Nursing, physical therapy	
6/10/97	Social isolation related to fatigue (p. 59)	Resident will participate in at least one group activity by 9/10/97 (p. 60)	1. Offer schedule of activities for resident to select choice(s) (p. 61) 2. Post personal activity schedule in resident's room (p. 61) 3. Take resident to at least one specific activity per week (p. 61) 4. Offer activity programs directed toward resident's specific interests (p. 62) 5. Select activities that allow for limited energy (p. 62)	Activities Activities Activities Activities Activities	

Reference

1. Morris, J. N., Flawes, K. M., Murphey, C. P., Nonemater, C. H., Phillips, S. N., Fries, B. F., and Moore, V. M. *Resident Assessment Instrument Training Manual and Resource Guide*. Natwick, MA: Elliot Press, 1991.

Chapter 1

Delirium

Definitions

Acute confusional state

Characterized by changes in consciousness, orientation, environmental awareness, and behavior

NANDA-Approved Nursing Diagnoses

Anxiety

Communication, impaired verbal

Confusion, acute

Physical mobility, impaired

Relocation stress syndrome

Self-care deficit

Sensory/perceptual alterations

Sleep pattern disturbance

Social interaction, impaired

Social isolation

Thought processes, altered

Problems/Needs

Easily distracted

Changing awareness of environment

Episodes of incoherent or disorganized speech

Restlessness

Lethargy

Varying mental function

Deteriorating intellectual function

Deteriorating ability to express information

Deteriorating ability to understand information

Deteriorating ability to hear information

Worsening of problem behavior (specify behavior)

Motor agitation (specify behavior, for example, pacing, handwringing, picking at real or imaginary objects)

Withdrawal from self-care activities

Withdrawal from leisure activities

Hallucinations

Delusions

Disorientation to time

Disorientation to time and place

Disorientation to time, place, and person

1. Delirium

Problems/Needs, continued

Decreased interest in personal, social, spiritual, and/or interpersonal activities

Fantasizing episodes

Unresponsive to environmental stimuli

Inappropriate verbal responses

Impaired thought processes

Sleep disturbance

Etiologies

Infection

Fecal impaction

Fever

Dehydration

Surgical trauma

Head trauma

Low blood sugar level

Inadequate respiratory function

Inadequate cardiac or circulatory function

Drug interaction

Medication side effects

Drug toxicity

Isolation

Recent loss of family/friend

Recent loss of money/abilities/home/pet/other

Use of physical restraints

Bowel or bladder urgency

Relocation

Hearing deficit

Visual deficit

Sensory deprivation

Sensory overload

Lack of sleep

Separation from loved ones

Change in life-style

Psychosocial distress

Depressed/sad or anxious mood

Pain

Multiple medications

Goals

The resident will:

Carry on conversation for _____ minutes by _____

Smile at _____ by _____

Initiate eye contact with another by _____

Maintain eye contact during a conversation by _____

State an interest in a brief activity by _____

Move body part in response to touch by _____

Respond to question or statement with appropriate verbalization by _____

Attend at least (number) _____ scheduled events without prompting by _____

Attend at least one group activity by _____

Remain at minimum of one group activity by _____

Participate in minimum of one group activity by _____

Follow one recommendation without prompting by _____

Allow another to complete task for self in area of intellectual deficit by _____

Make a noise when spoken to by _____

Become quiet when music is played by _____

Blink eyes in response to question by _____

Lie quietly when spoken to by _____

Open eyes when spoken to by _____

Repeat information as heard by _____

Repeat information as understood by _____

Sit erect and hold head up by _____

Read a sentence by _____

Verbalize positive feeling about body by _____

State all body parts belonging to own body by _____

Recognize body part as own by _____

Give abstract meaning of proverb or saying by _____

Explain logical progression of thought by _____

Sleep for (time) _____ by _____

Sleep peacefully for (time) _____ by _____

Sleep without having nightmare for (hours, days) _____ by _____

Express that paranoid feelings are inappropriate by _____

Distinguish self from others by _____

Distinguish self from objects by _____

Identify cause of paranoid feelings by _____

Display appropriate affect for situation by _____

Emphasize remaining strengths of self by _____

State remaining strengths of self by _____

Arrive at dining table before meal is served at least _____ % of time by _____

Read time on clock rather than asking what time it is by _____

Find own room without assistance at least _____ % of time by _____

Find dining room without assistance at least _____ % of time by _____

Find bathroom without assistance at least _____ % of time by _____

Show sign of recognizing (person) _____ by _____

Complete personal hygiene without assistance by _____

Put on own makeup by _____

Express desire for makeup to be applied by _____

Express desire to be clean-shaven by _____

Shave self without prompting by _____

Base statements in reality by _____

Base behavior in reality by _____

1. Delirium

Interventions

Provide 24-hour reality orientation

Ensure that resident has access to clock or watch at all times

Place calendar where resident has access to it

Encourage verbalization

Observe for changes in mental status

Encourage general hygiene self-care practices

Provide consistent caregiver

Approach resident warmly and positively

Respond to suspicious behavior in matter-of-fact and honest manner

Encourage resident to participate in activities

Encourage resident to perform at least _____ activities by self daily

Do not offer assistance for activity before resident attempts activity on own

Provide activities that require only short attention span for completion

Praise resident for completion of activity

Monitor drug levels through blood test results

Introduce resident to other residents on floor

Discuss feelings about placement in nursing home/in new room with resident

Keep environmental noises to a minimum

Provide at least _____ one-to-one session(s) with resident per day

Determine cause of hearing deficit

Monitor wax in ears

Check batteries in hearing aid

Place hearing aid in ear

Speak in lowered voice pitch

Increase volume of voice without shouting at resident

Touch resident to get resident's attention

Face resident when speaking to resident

Do not cover own mouth when speaking to resident

Do not stand in front of light source when speaking to resident (for example, window)

Encourage loved one(s) to visit resident at least

_____

Encourage loved one(s) to telephone resident at least

_____

Encourage loved one(s) to write resident at least

_____

Encourage loved one(s) to send tape recording to resident at least _____

Encourage loved one(s) to send video recording to resident at least _____

Establish daily routine with resident

Post daily routine in resident's room

Place resident in area of activity at least

_____

Discuss resident's feelings with resident

Determine interests of resident

Offer at least one activity to resident in which resident has shown interest

Discuss feelings of loss with resident

Assist resident in identifying areas of strengths for providing comfort

Allow resident to assist in choosing new room/roommate/nursing home

Orient resident to facility/new room/new roommate

Ensure that staff wear name tags at all times when caring for resident

Ensure that staff introduce themselves to resident at initiation of each interaction with resident

Write down instructions for resident to follow

Have resident repeat instructions

Refocus conversation with resident when resident expresses _____

Give medications as ordered for _____

Teach resident to _____

Instruct family/significant others to _____

Follow therapeutic regime for eliminating infection

Remove fecal impaction

Check for fecal impaction every _____

Ambulate resident every _____

Provide roughage in diet

Ensure that resident has liquid intake of at least _____ per _____

Follow postsurgical regime

Position resident to assure maximum respiratory exchange

Monitor resident for need of physical restraints

Remove physical restraints whenever possible

Place resident in restraint-reduction program

Change restraint to less restrictive device

Ensure that eyeglasses are in place/being worn by resident

Ensure that eyeglasses are appropriate strength/type for resident's needs

Repair eyeglasses

Provide assistance to resident in maintaining cleanliness of eyeglasses

Provide stimulation to resident through
_____

Talk with resident regarding strengths of new life-style

Monitor blood sugar levels every _____

Follow prescribed therapeutic diet

Alternate activity with rest periods

Allow no activity for 30 minutes after meals

Place resident in quiet environment

Place resident in activity where one person talks at a time

Eliminate all unnecessary medications

Give antianxiety medication when appropriate

Give sleeping medication when appropriate

Establish baseline for cognitive abilities

Review resident's drug profile with resident's physician

Chapter 2

Cognitive Loss/Dementia

Definition

Decline in intellectual functioning—often chronic and progressive

NANDA-Approved Nursing Diagnoses

Communication, impaired verbal

Confusion, chronic

Decreased adaptive capacity: intracranial

Environmental interpretation syndrome, impaired

Injury, high risk for

Memory, impaired

Role performance, altered

Social interaction, impaired

Thought processes, altered

Violence, high risk for: Self-directed or directed at others

Problems/Needs

Short-term memory deficit

Short-term and long-term memory deficit

Judgment deficit

Difficulty in making decisions

Unresponsive to environmental stimuli

Inappropriate verbal responses

Impaired thought processes

Misunderstands communication

Inappropriate motor responses (specify, for example, hitting, spitting, and so forth)

Does not understand communication

Disorientation to time

Disorientation to time and place

Disorientation to time, place, and person

2. Cognitive Loss/Dementia

Etiologies

Mental retardation

Brain damage

Brain deterioration

Mental illness

Sad mood

Mood decline

Constipation/fecal impaction

Inadequate cardiac function

Inadequate respiratory function

Low blood sugar

Inadequate thyroid function

Terminal prognosis

Pain

Infection

Decline in activities of daily living

Decline in continence

Drug interaction

Medication side effects

Drug toxicity

Multiple medications

Sensory deprivation

Hearing loss

Use of physical restraint

Visual distortion or loss

Goals

The resident will:

Find own room with/without cueing by _____

Find bathroom with/without cueing by _____

Find dining room with/without cueing by _____

Find daily schedule without assistance by _____

Identify (person) _____ by _____

Identify picture of _____ by _____

State birthdate/wedding anniversary date/maiden name by _____

Talk about past experiences by _____

Accept judgment of staff/significant other as appropriate by _____

Make a decision regarding clothing choice by _____

Make a decision regarding activity preference by _____

State a food preference by _____

Read time on clock rather than asking what time it is by _____

Repeat back information as understood by _____

Utilize environmental cues by _____

Respond to question/statement with appropriate verbalization by _____

Give abstract meaning of saying by _____

Explain logical progression of thought by _____

Emphasize remaining strengths of self by _____

Display appropriate response to situation by _____

Initiate eye contact with another by _____

Maintain eye contact during a conversation by _____

Sit erect and hold head up by _____

Carry on conversation for (time) _____ by _____

Complete requested task by _____

Demonstrate understanding by completing task by _____

Use communication book by _____

Demonstrate understanding by appropriately moving head/eyes in response to questions by _____

Move body part in response to touch by _____

Lie/sit quietly when music is played by _____

Blink eyes in response to question by _____

Lie quietly when spoken to by _____

Open eyes when spoken to by _____

Make noise when spoken to by _____

Refrain from hitting or spitting on another person by _____

Respond to question/statement by gestures by _____

Interventions

Provide 24-hour reality orientation

Ensure that resident has access to clock or watch at all times

Place calendar where resident has access to it

Observe for changes in cognitive status

Provide consistent caregiver

Approach resident warmly and positively

Monitor drug levels through blood test results

Provide at least _____ one-to-one session(s) with resident per day

Establish daily routine with resident

Post daily routine in resident's room

Provide activities that require only short attention span for completion

Place resident in area of activity at least _____ per day

Ensure that staff wear name tags at all times when caring for resident

Ensure that staff introduce themselves to resident at initiation of each interaction with resident

Write down instructions for resident to follow

Have resident repeat instructions

Repeat instructions several times

Give one instruction at a time to resident

Refocus conversation with resident when resident expresses _____

Give medications as ordered

Review resident's drug profile with resident's physician

Instruct family/significant others to _____

Position resident to ensure maximum respiratory exchange

Provide stimulation to resident through _____

Alternate activity with rest periods

2. Cognitive Loss/Dementia

Interventions, continued

Allow no activity for 30 minutes after meals

Use gestures as part of communication

Ignore inappropriate actions

Gently redirect activities when resident

Repeat communication using more than one communication method (words, gestures, facial expressions)

Explain each activity/care procedure prior to beginning it

Maintain eye contact with resident while talking with resident

Touch resident on hand at beginning of each interaction

Communicate with resident in quiet environment

Tell resident that behavior is inappropriate

Place resident in behavior modification program

Praise resident for appropriate verbal response

Praise resident for each decision made

Give resident two choices when presenting decisions

Offer simple choices to resident

Give resident no choice that will be overwhelming

Modify environment to prevent situations that trigger inappropriate behavior

Use physical restraints when appropriate

Use least restrictive physical restraint possible

Place resident on restraint reduction program

Use nonverbal communication techniques to encourage resident response

Break activities into manageable subtasks

Provide verbal reminders to resident

Encourage small-group activities

Ensure that glasses are clean and in place

Ask physician to order eye examination

Establish toileting routine

Follow toileting routine

Check for fecal impaction (frequency)

Monitor fluid intake

Chapter 3

Visual Function

Definition

Ability to focus on objects, discriminate color, and adjust to changes in light and dark

NANDA-Approved Nursing Diagnoses

Sensory/perceptual alterations: Visual

Problems/Needs

Decreased vision

Blindness

Eye pain

Blurry vision

Double vision

Impaired side vision

Impaired central vision

Etiologies

Eye medications

Decreased pupil size

Increased pupil size

Clinical eye complications

Cataracts

Nonuse of eyeglasses

Ill-fitting eyeglasses

Broken eyeglasses

Incorrect lens prescription

Lack of eyeglasses

Inability to put on/maintain eyeglasses

Medication side effects

Infection

Removal of eye

Head trauma

Eye trauma

3. Visual Function

Goals

The resident will:

Use compensatory mechanism for decreased vision by _____

Wear eyeglasses routinely by _____

Ask staff to put on/clean eyeglasses for resident by _____

Obtain eyeglasses by _____

Have eyeglasses adjusted by _____

Prevent breakage of eyeglasses by appropriate maintenance/storage by _____

Show no signs of infection in eyes by _____

Cooperate during eye exam by _____

State blurry vision has improved/cleared by _____

State decrease in eye pain by _____

State decrease/elimination of double vision by _____

Demonstrate compensatory way to deal with impaired side vision by _____

Demonstrate compensatory way to deal with impaired central vision by _____

Demonstrate compensation for increased light entering eye by _____

Demonstrate compensation for decreased light entering eye by _____

Not reinjure eye by _____

Interventions

Ensure that eyeglasses are in place/being worn by resident

Ensure that eyeglasses are appropriate strength/type for resident's needs

Obtain eye exam for resident

Obtain eyeglasses for resident

Repair resident's eyeglasses

Provide assistance to resident in maintaining cleanliness of eyeglasses

Allow eye ointment to become transparent before resident undertakes activity

Teach resident to turn head from side to side when walking/using wheelchair

Have resident use visor to shade eyes

Place resident away from glare when need for visual acuity

Position window blinds to decrease glare

Have resident wear sunglasses at all times

Provide light for reading from lamp placed behind resident's shoulder

Use large-print material with resident

Teach resident good hygienic practices

Teach resident to wash hands after touching infected eye

Teach resident not to rub one eye and then other eye

Provide care of eye trauma

Follow head trauma therapeutic regime

Follow eye trauma therapeutic regime

Provide care for eye prosthesis

Evaluate need for medication causing eye side effect(s)

Provide Braille material for resident

Enroll resident in Braille reading class

Teach resident to move head from side to side when eating

Focus resident's vision on object to side of center

Instill/apply eye medication as ordered

Refer resident to low-vision services

Place large-print sign identifying resident's room

Do not rearrange furniture in resident's environment

Train resident to use cane to recognize objects in path

Post "blind" or "vision-impaired" signs in resident's room and outside door to resident's room (if allowed by regulatory agencies)

Store resident's eyeglasses at nurses' station at night

Leave night light on during the night

Color code hallways/door entries/other

Use telephone with large numbers

Use 300-watt bulb in reading lamp

Chapter 4

Communication

Definition

Ability to express emotion, listen to others, and share information

NANDA-Approved Nursing Diagnoses

Communication, impaired verbal

Sensory/perceptual alterations

Problems/Needs

Decreased hearing

Does not speak

Receptive aphasia (does not understand verbal and/or written communication)

Expressive aphasia (inability to express thoughts verbally and/or in writing)

Whispered speech

Difficulty pronouncing words

Slurred speech

Difficulty finding words

Impaired communication

Incoherent speech

Inappropriate speech

Inappropriate verbal response

Inability to understand others

Inability to make self understood

4. Communication

Etiologies

Decline in cognitive status

Hearing deficit

Visual deficit

Earwax accumulation

Ear infection

Psychiatric disorder

Medication side effects

Drug toxicity

Multiple medications

Muscle paralysis

Muscle weakness

Involuntary movements of tongue

Nonuse of hearing aid/other assistive device

Goals

The resident will:

Show no signs of ear infection by _____

Show no signs of earwax accumulation by _____

Demonstrate ability to hear by answering question appropriately by _____

Demonstrate understanding by completing task when requested by _____

Speak in a manner that can be understood by _____

Use communication book appropriately by _____

Use writing as a means of communicating by _____

Pronounce words correctly by _____

Show a decrease/elimination of slurring when speaking by _____

Use gestures to supplement communication by _____

Use nonverbal communication techniques by _____

Carry on appropriate conversation by _____

Use touch in communicating by _____

Maintain eye contact while conversing by _____

Face person with whom resident is conversing by _____

Reduce background noise while conversing by _____

Say at least (number) _____ of words coherently by _____

Answer question appropriately by _____

Utilize an alternative method of communication by _____

Say at least one complete sentence by _____

Use assistive device by _____

Interventions

Refer resident to speech therapist for evaluation

Provide mirror so that resident can view process while practicing speech

Praise efforts when resident _____

Ask resident questions that require one- or two-word answers

Ensure that resident attends speech therapy _____ times per _____

Watch resident's mouth when resident is speaking

Ensure that speaker's face is in light when speaking

Encourage resident to pronounce words slowly

Encourage resident to enunciate each word clearly

Do not stand in front of light source when conversing with resident

Touch resident before beginning to speak to resident

Face resident when speaking to resident

Do not cover own mouth when speaking to resident

Teach resident how to use communication book

Teach resident how to use communication board

Teach resident how to use electronic communication device

Remove as much background noise as possible when speaking with resident

Move resident to low-noise place before speaking with resident

Monitor exercises _____ times per

_____

Teach resident to _____

Instruct family/significant others to _____

Encourage nonverbal communication with resident

Disregard inappropriate words when resident is conversing

Place ear close to resident's mouth when listening to resident

Check for wax in resident's ears

Ensure that wax is removed from ears

Treat ear infection as ordered

Monitor drug level of medications with toxicity to ears

Monitor for side effects of medications with ear implications

Monitor for side effects of medications with eye implications

Monitor cognitive status

Use short, direct phrases when talking with resident

Refer for audiology evaluation

Teach resident to use assistive device

Instruct family in correct use of assistive device by resident

Praise resident for use of assistive device

Chapter 5

ADL Functional/Rehabilitation Potential: Mobility

Definition

ADL (activities of daily living) functional potential—potential to perform the following functions: mobility (bed, transfer, locomotion), dressing, eating, toilet use, personal hygiene, and bathing

Rehabilitation potential—potential to restore function to maximum self-sufficiency

NANDA-Approved Nursing Diagnosis

Disuse syndrome, risk for

Peripheral neurovascular dysfunction, risk for

Perioperative positioning injury, risk for

Physical mobility, impaired

Problems/Needs

Impaired mobility

Joint contracture

Inability to walk

Inability to transfer to (specify, for example, chair, toilet, tub, and so forth)

Inability to propel own wheelchair

Immobility in bed

Bedfast

Inability to move body part (specify)

Inability to move body part without assistance

Inability to move body part without direction

Potential for injury

Limited joint range of motion

Limited active joint range of motion

Poor tolerance of walking

Impaired coordination

Imposed restrictions of movement

Leans consistently

5. ADL Functional/Rehabilitation Potential: Mobility

Etiologies

Inability to move independently

Lack of trunk/limb control

Muscle weakness

Limited range of motion

Poor coordination

Environmental barriers

Lack of self-confidence

Poor balance

Decreased arm strength

Decreased strength in lower extremities

Impaired arm mobility

Inability to use one arm

Impaired mobility of lower extremities

Cognitive impairment

General debilitation

Recovering from illness

Recovering from surgery

Injury of (specify) _____

Lack of sensation in body part (specify)

_____

Decreased visual acuity

Refusal to move joint

Inability to move joint

Decreased inhibition of flexor muscles

Drop in blood pressure with certain movements

Low blood pressure

Visual field loss

Knowledge deficit

Pain

Splinting of joint

Casting of joint

Joint/limb edema

Use of physical restraint

Use of sedating or tranquilizing medication

Fatigue

Lethargy

Depression

Anxiety

Instability in health condition

Terminal prognosis

Loss of position sense

Goals

The resident will:

Propel own wheelchair _____ feet by _____

Transfer self to tub without assistance by _____

Transfer self to toilet without assistance by _____

Transfer self to tub with assistance of (device/person) _____ by _____

Transfer self to toilet with assistance of (device/person) _____ by _____

Walk _____ feet without assistance by _____

Walk _____ feet with assistance of (device/person) _____ by _____

Move about in bed without assistance by _____

Move about in bed with assistance of (device/person) _____ by _____

Tolerate sitting in chair for five minutes by _____

Be out of bed for _____ minutes per day by _____

Be out of bed for _____ minutes _____ times a day by _____

Have body part repositioned (frequency) _____ by _____

Reposition own body part by _____

Move own body part by _____

Increase passive joint range of motion by _____

Increase active joint range of motion by _____

Demonstrate increased muscle strength of (identify area) _____ by _____

Show improved coordination of (identify body parts) _____ by _____

Comply with restrictions of movement of (identify body parts) _____ by _____

Maintain angle of joint contracture by _____

Maintain upright posture by _____

Not fall by _____

Not receive injury in fall by _____

Have no more than _____ falls per _____ by _____

Maintain current mobility status by _____

Improve angle of joint contracture by _____ degrees by _____

Transfer self with assistance of (device/person) _____ by _____

Transfer self without assistance by _____

Show a reduction of joint/limb edema by _____

Have resolution of joint/limb edema by _____

State that pain is present less than _____ percent of time by _____

State that no pain is present when (specify activity) _____ by _____

State that ambulation is desired by _____

5. ADL Functional/Rehabilitation Potential: Mobility

Interventions

Encourage resident to propel own wheelchair _____ feet (frequency) _____

Ambulate with assistance of (number of people, device) _____

Teach resident to transfer from _____ to _____ with assistance of (number of persons/device) _____

Teach resident to maintain position in chair by placing (pillows, poseys, and so forth) _____ (where) _____

Teach resident to use (specify assistive device) _____ when transferring/ambulating/repositioning

Observe resident for signs of fatigue when sitting in chair

Teach resident to push wheelchair to destination

Reposition resident (frequency) _____ per day with assistance of (number of persons/device) _____

Enforce ordered mobility restrictions (specify restrictions) _____

Assess for need of assistive device (specify) _____

Assess for proper use of assistive device

Show resident how to position body part in position (specify) _____ when in bed

Show resident how to position own body part in position (specify) _____ when in chair

Show resident how to position body part in position (specify) _____ when transferring

Give resident passive range of motion to joints (specify) _____ (frequency) _____

Supervise active range of motion to joints (specify) _____ (frequency) _____

Provide assisted active range of motion to joints (specify) _____ (frequency)

Have resident attempt all movements by self before offering assistance

Have resident complete _____ movements before giving assistance

Reinforce use of assistive device (specify) _____

Praise resident after attempt to (specify) _____

Praise resident after completing (specify) _____

Refer to (specify physician or therapist) _____ for evaluation

Give verbal cues to resident regarding (specify) _____

Have resident use safety devices (specify) _____ with activity (specify) _____

Provide complete range-of-motion exercises with joint(s) submerged in warm water

Give pain-relieving medication (timing) _____ before activity (specify) _____

Observe ambulation for endurance

Observe ambulation for steadiness

Teach resident to _____

Instruct family/significant others to _____

Ambulate resident with assistance of (device/number of people) _____ (feet)_____ (frequency) _____

Encourage resident to ambulate independently _____ feet (frequency) _____

Refer resident for physical therapy evaluation

Follow physical therapy regime for resident

Use pain-relieving device (specify) _____ (frequency) _____

Place resident in mobility-restorative program

Comply with mobility-restorative program

Ensure that corns are trimmed (frequency) _____

Apply (specify) _____ prosthesis before _____

Position (specify joint) _____ in position of comfort

Reposition (specify joint) _____ every _____

Support (specify limb/joint) _____ with use of _____ for (time) _____ every _____

Support (specify limb/joint) _____ with use of _____ when _____

Teach resident to walk next to railing/use railing in hallways

Do not allow resident to ambulate without assistance

Measure and record (specify joint) _____ angle every _____

Elevate (specify joint/limb) _____ on _____ for _____ every _____

Record number of falls

Analyze falls for trend or pattern

Inspect resident closely for injury after each fall

Teach resident how to protect self when falling

Use safety appliance (specify) _____ to help prevent falls

Measure and record edema of _____ every _____

Record amount of time resident states he/she is in pain

Observe resident for expressions of pain

Observe resident for expressions of pain during _____

Teach resident to move head from side to side for side vision while walking/eating

Take blood pressure in reclining position and then in sitting position

Take blood pressure in sitting position and then in standing position

Remind resident not to stand in one place for prolonged period of time

Place eyeglasses on resident prior to walking

Test extremities for presence of sensation

Turn resident on side (number of times) _____ per _____

Reposition resident every _____

Inspect limb stump for signs of skin breakdown every _____

Pad prosthesis with _____ before applying to resident

Soak clenched fists in warm water for _____ every _____

Apply dry, rolled washcloth between fingers and palm (when) _____

Dry palms of hands and fingers well after each bath/soak

Apply support hose as ordered

Apply elastic support bandage as ordered

Remove environmental barriers for mobility

Place in restraint-reduction program

Attempt use of alternate devices prior to restraints

Provide alternating periods of rest and activity

Have resident rest for 30 minutes after each meal

Clear path of objects prior to ambulating resident

5. ADL Functional/Rehabilitation Potential: Dressing

NANDA-Approved Nursing Diagnosis

Self-care deficit, dressing/grooming

Problems/Needs

Inability to put on necessary items of clothing

Inability to take off necessary items of clothing

Impaired ability to fasten clothing (for example, snaps, zippers, buttons, and so forth)

Impaired ability to tie shoes

Inappropriate choice of types of clothing

Inappropriate choice of amount of clothing

Inappropriate choice of combinations of clothing

Inappropriate removal of own clothing

Inability to locate appropriate clothing

Inability to appropriately sequence dressing

Etiologies

Impaired mobility of arms

Impaired mobility of fingers

Impaired mobility of hands

Decreased strength in arms

Decreased strength in hands

Poor balance

Involuntary movements

Decreased visual acuity

Visual field deficit

Cognitive impairment

Short attention span

Agitation

Difficulty in making decisions

Impaired judgment

Apathy

Easy fatigability

Inappropriate expression of sexual needs

Poor short-term memory

Goals

The resident will:

Put on at least one item of clothing without assistance by _____

Put on at least one item of clothing with assistance of (person/device) _____ by _____

Take off at least one item of clothing without assistance by _____

Take off at least one item of clothing with assistance of (person/device) _____ by _____

Fasten at least one snap/hook on clothing by _____

Pull up zipper on clothing by _____

Be appropriately dressed with assistance by _____

Be appropriately dressed without assistance by _____

Choose one appropriate item of clothing to wear each day by _____

Wear one layer of clothing at a time by _____

Pick out one complete appropriate outfit to wear by _____

Tie own shoes with assistance of (person/device) _____ by _____

Tie own shoes without assistance by _____

Leave clothing on for (amount of time) _____ by _____

Maintain ability for self-dressing without assistance by _____

(Specify activity) _____ with supervision by _____

(Specify activity) _____ without supervision by _____

(Specify activity) _____ with verbal prompting by _____

(Specify activity) _____ without verbal prompting by _____

Locate appropriate clothing to be put on by _____

Put clothes on in correct order by _____

Dress self with clothing without fasteners by _____

5. ADL Functional/Rehabilitation Potential: Dressing

Interventions

Select appropriate clothing for resident

Assist resident in selecting clothing

Supervise resident in dressing

Give standby assistance to resident when dressing

Give verbal cues to resident when dressing

Dress resident completely

Break dressing into subtasks

Give one instruction at a time

Place resident in quiet environment for dressing

Place resident in dressing-restorative program

Give assistance to resident in dressing only after resident has attempted each step

Ensure that resident's clothing is clean

Ensure that resident has seasonally appropriate clothing

Provide clothing to resident that has easy-to-handle fasteners, such as Velcro

Provide clothing to resident that has no fasteners

Provide active assistive range of motion to (joint) _____ (frequency) _____

Assist resident with strengthening exercises (specify type and frequency) _____

Praise resident for each completed step in dressing

Praise resident for each completed step in undressing

Assist resident with fine motor movement exercises for the hands/fingers (specify type and frequency) _____

Lead resident through specified active range of motion of joint (specify) _____

Refer for occupational therapy evaluation

Implement dressing-restorative program for resident

Supervise hand/arm strengthening exercises (frequency) _____

Refer for eye exam

Ensure that eyeglasses are in place, clean, and appropriate for resident

Alternate rest and segment of dressing

Give resident limited choices in clothing selection

Place resident in area where constant observation is possible when undressing occurs

Remove resident from public area when undressing occurs

Replace removed clothing on resident

Remove resident from public area when behavior is unacceptable

Dress resident in clothing that is difficult for resident to remove

Position resident so that dressing can occur while resident is in secure (balanced) position

Provide privacy for sexual activity

Provide time alone with spouse or significant other without interruption

Use gentle, firm approach with resident

5. ADL Functional/Rehabilitation Potential: Eating

NANDA-Approved Nursing Diagnosis

Self-care deficit, feeding

Swallowing, impaired

Problems/Needs

Inability to chew properly

Does not convey food into mouth

Difficulty swallowing food/liquids

Inability to cut food

Inability to use eating utensils

Chokes easily

Aspirates food easily

Eats very slowly

Etiologies

Easy fatigability

Poor dentition

Edentulousness

Eats food rapidly

Inability to cut food into small pieces

Impaired arm mobility

Impaired arm strength

Impaired hand mobility

Impaired hand strength

Improperly fitting/broken dentures

Improperly fitting/broken partial plate

Sore in mouth

Sore throat

Muscular paralysis

Muscular weakness

Choking

Dislike of food(s) (specify) _____

Allergy to food(s) (specify) _____

Enjoys eating

Eats in response to mood

Feelings of anger

Nausea

Vomiting

Cognitive impairment

Goals

The resident will:

Eat _____ % of one meal by _____

Eat _____ % of each meal by _____

Eat at least one-third of each food served per meal by _____

Eat at least _____ % of _____ meals per day by _____

Not aspirate any food by _____

Convey food to own mouth by _____

Swallow foods served at meals by _____

State feeling of fullness after meals by _____

Cut own food by _____

Use eating utensils properly by _____

Finish each meal by the time all other residents have left dining area by _____

Choke fewer than _____ times per meal by _____

Choke fewer than _____ times per day by _____

Choke fewer than _____ times per week by _____

Maintain current eating level by _____

Use at least one eating utensil appropriately by _____

5. ADL Functional/Rehabilitation Potential: Eating

Interventions

Give food that is easily swallowed by resident

Give food that is easily chewed by resident

Hand-feed resident

Use appropriate devices, (specify) _____, to assist resident to feed self

Elevate head of bed at least _____ degrees while eating

Elevate head of bed at least _____ degrees for at least _____ hours after eating

Elevate head of bed at least _____ degrees at all times

Keep resident up in chair _____ (time) after meals

Maintain pleasant environment at mealtimes

Allow resident extra time to eat

Instruct resident to avoid snacking within one hour of mealtime

Reinforce that resident should eat slowly

Feed resident slowly

Stimulate swallowing with spoon or by stroking resident's throat

Suction resident when needed

Refer resident to occupational therapist for evaluation and recommendations

Refer resident to physical therapist for evaluation and recommendations

Place resident in eating-restorative program

Ensure that dentures are in place

Use appropriate devices, (specify) _____, to assist in prevention of choking

Assign only staff who have been trained in Heimlich maneuver to work with resident in eating

Refer to dental hygienist/dentist for evaluation and recommendations

Provide foods/liquids soothing to sore oropharyngeal structures

Teach resident to _____

Instruct family/significant others to _____

Cut food for resident

Eliminate odors from eating area

Document allergy to food(s) in all appropriate areas

Check tray to ensure that food to which resident is allergic has not been placed on tray

Eliminate food causing adverse effects

Offer substitutes for uneaten foods

Ask family to bring preferred foods to resident

Refer to dietitian for evaluation and recommendations

Provide nondistracting eating environment

Remain with resident during meals

Remove resident from dining area immediately following meals

Provide socialization with meals

Place resident at meals with residents who have similar interests

Place resident at meals with residents who have aesthetically pleasant eating manners

Determine resident's food preferences and dislikes

Monitor abdomen for distention

Monitor bowel sounds daily

Assist resident with eating when resident becomes fatigued

Offer ground meat with diet

Evaluate medications that may be causing nausea/vomiting/other side effects

Complete swallowing evaluation

5. ADL Functional/Rehabilitation Potential: Toileting

NANDA-Approved Nursing Diagnosis

Self-care deficit, toileting

Problems/Needs

Ineffective bowel elimination

Inability to transfer to stool/commode

Diarrhea

Constipation/fecal impaction

Etiologies

Cognitive impairment

Lack of sensation of bowel fullness

Anxiety

Infection

Increased abdominal pressure

Unwillingness to remain on stool/commode until elimination process is completed

Use of laxative/cathartic

Absence of routine

Decreased arm strength

Decrease strength in lower extremities

Impaired arm mobility

Impaired mobility of lower extremities

General debilitation

Lack of sensation in arms/legs

Poor balance

Pain

Fatigue

Lethargy

Use of medication that causes (specify) (e.g., constipation, muscle weakness, poor balance, diarrhea, other) _____

Colostomy

Food(s) that cause (specify) (e.g., constipation, diarrhea, other)_____

Anal/rectal fissure/sore

Hemorrhoids

Goals

The resident will:

Learn/state one mechanism for communicating the need to have bowel movement by _____

Ask for a laxative only every _____ days by _____

Ask for an enema only every _____ days by _____

Have no pain with bowel movement by _____

State that bowels have not moved for (specify) _____ days by _____

Have no involuntary passage of stool by _____

Have no more than (number) _____ involuntary stools by _____

Remain continent of bowels by _____

Cooperate in establishing a routine for bowel elimination by _____

Ask for assistance in transferring to stool/commode by _____

Remain on stool/commode until elimination process is completed by _____

Position self on stool/commode by _____

Open/remove clothing in preparation for elimination by _____

Have properly functioning colostomy by _____

Have a decrease/elimination of diarrhea by _____

Have an established bowel routine by _____

Show a decrease in number/frequency of fecal impactions by _____

State a decreased feeling of constipation by _____

5. ADL Functional/Rehabilitation Potential: Toileting

Interventions

Monitor abdomen for distention (frequency) _____

Monitor bowel sounds (frequency) _____

Check resident for fecal impaction (frequency) _____

Monitor intervals between bowel movements

Provide nondistracting toileting environment

Evaluate need for medication that causes (specify) _____

Discuss substitute for medication that causes (specify) _____

Evaluate resident's bowel control and pattern

Establish bowel routine for resident

Check rectum (frequency) _____ for presence and amount of stool

Manually evacuate stool

Place in bowel-restorative program

Use incontinent briefs as needed

Do not use incontinent briefs on resident

Medicate with (name and frequency) _____ as ordered

Apply external medication (name and frequency) _____ as ordered

Offer bedpan (frequency) _____

Take resident to bathroom (frequency or timing) _____

Offer resident (number) _____ glasses of fluids per (day/shift) _____

Set up communication mechanism with resident regarding toileting

Change colostomy bag as needed (frequency/when) _____

Change colostomy appliance as needed (frequency/when) _____

Observe ostomy site for signs of infection such as inflammation, drainage, and odor

Irrigate colostomy every _____

Remove hard stool from colostomy manually

Give resident _____ ounces of prune juice per _____

Give (type) _____ enema (frequency) _____

Give (type) _____ suppository (frequency) _____

Give (type) _____ laxative (frequency) _____

Give (amount) _____ bran every morning

Give (amount) _____ hot water _____ (times) every day

Remind resident to tell staff if resident has had bowel movement

Evaluate resident's bowel function

Ask resident/significant others what aids best assist with resident's bowel function

Evaluate perianal region for hemorrhoids, fistulas, fissures, and so forth

Eliminate foods causing adverse effects (diarrhea/constipation)

Provide clear liquid diet for (time) _____

Advance diet as tolerated by resident

Remove stress causing diarrhea from environment

Allow resident to rest prior to attempt at toileting

Position on bedpan comfortably

Position on bedpan in upright position

Assist resident to stool/commode (frequency) _____

Monitor strengthening exercises for arms/legs (frequency) _____

Monitor mobility exercises for arms/legs (frequency) _____

Medicate for pain as ordered

Place resident in whirlpool/tub with warm water (frequency, timing) _____

5. ADL Functional/Rehabilitation Potential: Personal Hygiene

NANDA-Approved Nursing Diagnoses

Self-care deficit, bathing/hygiene

Self-care deficit, dressing/grooming

Problems/Needs

Inability to shave self

Inability to apply own makeup

Inability to comb/brush hair

Impaired ability to clean/polish shoes

Inability to clean/brush teeth/dentures

Spills food/fluids on clothing

Inability to maintain appearance at satisfactory level

Inability to shampoo hair

Scaling scalp

Etiologies

Decreased visual acuity

Muscle weakness

Involuntary muscle movements

Easy fatigability

Lethargy

Unwillingness to perform task

Impaired arm/hand mobility

Inability to scrub scalp

Poor coordination

Lack of ability to sequence task steps

Unavailability of needed supplies

Poor attention span

Poor short-term memory

Cognitive deficit

Lack of interest in appearance

Goals

The resident will:

Shave self with/without assistance by _____

Shave self with verbal prompting by _____

Put on own makeup by _____

Express desire for makeup to be applied by _____

Express desire for hair to be combed/brushed by _____

Express desire to be clean-shaven by _____

Clean/polish shoes with/without assistance by _____

Clean/polish shoes with verbal prompting by _____

Express desire to have teeth/dentures cleaned/brushed by _____

Clean/brush teeth/dentures with/without assistance by _____

Have minimal number of food stains on clothing after one meal by _____

Have minimal number of food stains on clothing at end of day by _____

Have no food stains on clothing at end of day by _____

Express desire for hair to be shampooed by _____

Shampoo hair with/without assistance by _____

Have minimal/no scaling of scalp by _____

5. ADL Functional/Rehabilitation Potential: Personal Hygiene

Interventions

Place shaver in resident's hand

Position resident in front of mirror

Place makeup appliance in resident's hand

Praise resident for each completed step in personal hygiene

Give verbal cues to resident while grooming

Set utensils needed for grooming within easy reach of resident

Place comb in resident's hand

Place brush in resident's hand

Obtain shoelaces that are pretied

Obtain slip-on shoes for resident

Obtain old pair of shoes for resident to practice polishing

Put toothpaste on toothbrush for resident

Place toothbrush in resident's hand

Ensure that resident's clothing is covered during mealtime

Ensure that eyeglasses are in place, properly fitting, properly maintained, and with proper prescription

Alternate rest periods with grooming activity

Discuss portions of tasks that resident would be willing to attempt

Monitor arm/hand mobility exercises (frequency)

Place shampoo on resident's hair/in resident's hand

Place resident's hands on scalp

Provide needed grooming supplies to resident

Provide verbal cueing for grooming task

Praise resident for his/her appearance when appropriate

Provide nondistracting environment for grooming

Place resident in grooming-restorative program

5. ADL Functional/Rehabilitation Potential: Bathing

NANDA-Approved Nursing Diagnosis

Self-care deficit, bathing/hygiene

Problems/Needs

Inability to wash body or body parts

Inability to bathe independently

Resists bathing

Forgets to bathe

Inability to dry body or body parts

Inability to judge water temperature

Etiologies

Cognitive impairment

Impaired mobility

Decreased strength

Allergy to soap

Short attention span

Inability to complete task independently

Change in established routine

Resistance to bathing

Short-term memory deficit

Fear of (specify) _____

Goals

The resident will:

Bathe at scheduled times for _____ consecutive weeks by _____

Bathe at scheduled times without resistance by _____

Bathe at least one limb of body independently by _____

Maintain independent self-bathing by _____

Bathe at least (specify body area) _____ independently by _____

Bathe self with supervision by _____

Dry at least one limb of body independently by _____

Ask staff person to check water temperature before bathing by _____

Correctly read thermometer in checking water temperature before bathing by _____

5. ADL Functional/Rehabilitation Potential: Bathing

Interventions

Evaluate resident's ability to bathe self

Assist resident with bathing as needed

Post bathing schedule in resident's room

Discuss bathing schedule with resident

Give verbal reminder to resident to bathe on scheduled bath days

Supervise resident during bathing

Stay with resident during bathing

Give verbal cues to resident during bathing

Wash hair with special shampoo (specify) _____ (frequency) _____

Use gentle, firm approach to get resident to bathe

Note if resident bathes self without assistance or supervision

Teach resident to _____

Instruct family/significant others to _____

Document allergy to soap in appropriate places

Do not use soap for bathing resident

Set water temperature for resident

Obtain water thermometer for resident to use prior to bathing

Demonstrate bathing techniques to resident

Position resident so self-bathing/drying can occur

Monitor hand/finger strengthening exercises (frequency) _____

Praise all efforts made by resident to bathe

Remind resident of change in bathing schedule

Place resident in bathing-restorative program

Chapter 6

Urinary Incontinence and Indwelling Catheter

Definition

Inability to control urination

NANDA-Approved Nursing Diagnoses

Incontinence, functional

Incontinence, reflex

Incontinence, stress

Incontinence, total

Incontinence, urge

Infection, risk for

Urinary elimination, altered

Urinary retention

Problems/Needs

Inability to communicate need to urinate

Intermittent dribbling of urine

Continuous dribbling of urine

Inability to control urination after need to urinate is identified

Inability to sense need to urinate

Stress incontinence

Urinates small amounts frequently

Painful urination

Potential for urinary tract infection

Urinary tract infection

Potential for self-transmitted infection

Potential for injury

6. Urinary Incontinence and Indwelling Catheter

Etiologies

Impaired speech

Aphasia

Delirium

Depression

Cognitive impairment

Loss of bladder muscle tone

Loss of sphincter control

Inability to empty bladder completely

Bladder spasms

Impaired mobility

Anxiety

Fear of incontinence

Infection

Increased abdominal pressure

Unwillingness to remain on stool/commode until elimination process is completed

Poor hygienic techniques

Absence of routine

Immobility

Lack of access to toilet/commode

Fecal impaction

High blood sugar

Pedal edema

Use of diuretics

Use of sedatives/hypnotics/other medication

Pain related to urination

Inadequate fluid intake

Excessive fluid intake

Lack of control of clinical condition (specify)
_____

Inadequate urine output

Atrophic vaginitis

High blood calcium

Vitamin B_{12} deficiency

Short-term memory deficit

Environmental barriers to stool/commode

Use of physical restraints

Comatose condition

Return of urine into bladder from tubing

Inadequate drainage of urine from bladder

Collection of deposits in bladder or catheter

Frequent catheter manipulation

Forcible removal of catheter by resident

Alkalinity of urine

Use of leg bag for urine collection

Presence of indwelling catheter

Goals

The resident will:

Be able to correctly judge need to urinate by _____

Remain continent by _____

Be incontinent no more than _____ times per _____ by _____

Learn one mechanism for communicating the need to urinate to a staff person by _____

Have no pain on urination by _____

Increase the amount of urine voided by _____ ml per _____ by _____

Remain continent of bladder by _____

Increase fluid intake to _____ glasses per day by _____

Show no sign of urinary tract infection by _____

Establish a routine for urine elimination by _____

Maintain acidic urine for _____ days by _____

Use proper hygienic practices by _____

Be free of urinary tract pain for at least (time)
_____ by _____

Receive no injury secondary to catheter manipulation
by _____

Receive no injury secondary to catheter removal by resident by _____

Cooperate with catheter therapeutic regime by
_____

Cooperate in establishing a routine for urine elimination by _____

Ask for assistance in transferring to stool/commode by
_____

Ask for removal of environmental barriers to reaching
stool/commode by _____

Remain on stool/commode until elimination process is
completed by _____

Position self on stool/commode by _____

Open/remove clothing in preparation for elimination by
_____

Cooperate in therapeutic regime by _____

Limit intake of fluid to _____ after
_____ (time) by _____

Use urinal when in bed/at night by _____

Interventions

Implement bladder program

Use incontinent briefs on resident as needed

Do not use incontinent briefs on resident

Change incontinent briefs (frequency) _____

Give perineal care when resident is incontinent

Place urinal within resident's reach

Stay with resident while resident is on stool/commode

Apply pressure over suprapubic area at end of urination
to assist in bladder evacuation

Evaluate resident's bladder control and pattern

Establish bladder routine for resident

Use verbal reminders for urine control

Use verbal reminders for fecal control

Offer bedpan (frequency) _____

Request that resident tell staff when signs of urinary
tract infection occur (frequency, urgency, blood in
urine, painful urination, and so forth)

Take resident to bathroom (frequency)
_____

Offer resident (number) _____ glasses of fluids per
(day and shift) _____

Keep stress to a minimum to decrease incontinence

Set up communication mechanism with resident regarding toileting

Use nonverbal communication techniques with resident
to indicate toileting/need for toileting

Use communication book/device/board/writing to indicate need for toileting

Teach resident importance of emptying bladder
completely

Check rectum (frequency) _____ for
presence and amount of stool

Manually evacuate stool (frequency) _____

6. Urinary Incontinence and Indwelling Catheter

Interventions, continued

Teach resident to _____

Instruct family/significant others to _____

Give medication as ordered for bladder spasms

Medicate with (name and frequency) _____ as ordered

Evaluate effectiveness and side effects of medications (name) _____

Follow therapeutic regime for control of blood sugar

Tell resident what care will be given prior to initiating the care

Follow therapeutic regime for elimination of urinary tract infection

Take resident to bathroom following every meal

Place commode in resident's room

Place urinal within resident's reach

Place bedpan within resident's reach

Follow therapeutic regime for atrophic vaginitis

Follow therapeutic regime for elevating _____

Follow therapeutic regime for lowering _____

Follow therapeutic regime for eliminating _____

Remove environmental barriers to stool/commode access

Place resident in wheelchair/use walker to get to bathroom

Toilet resident every 1 to 2 hours when restraint removed

Discontinue use of diuretics as soon as possible (or decrease dosage, amount, and so forth)

Follow restricted fluid intake regime as ordered

Change catheter (frequency) _____

Tape catheter to (area) _____

Place mitt restraints on resident's hands when _____

Use wrist restraints on resident when resident pulls on catheter

Inflate catheter balloon with (number) _____ ml of _____

Irrigate catheter (frequency) _____ with _____

Medicate resident with (name and frequency) _____

Offer resident acid ash drinks, (for example, cranberry juice), _____, (frequency) _____ times a day

Use urine collection leg bag only when resident is sitting, standing, or walking

Position urine collection bag below level of bladder

Position catheter tubing below level of bladder

Position resident so urine will drain from bladder

Check tubing for kinks (frequency) _____

Insert (size) _____ catheter

Insert indwelling catheter

Catheterize resident intermittently as ordered

Provide relaxing atmosphere for urination

Allow resident to remain on stool/commode for up to (time)_____

Encourage resident to urinate while sitting in warm water

Pour warm water over perineum prior to/during urination

Give pain medication as ordered

Give pain medication 30 minutes prior to toileting resident

Walk resident to stool/commode _____ times per day

Institute distracting activity for resident when resident wants to leave stool/commode prior to completion of urination

Offer bedpan/stool/commode more frequently after diuretic given/feet elevated

Review successful continence with resident

Chapter 7

Psychosocial Well-Being

Definition

Feelings regarding self and social relationships

NANDA-Approved Nursing Diagnoses

Adjustment, impaired

Anxiety

Body image disturbance

Decisional conflict

Defensive coping

Denial, ineffective

Family coping, compromised, ineffective

Fear

Grieving, dysfunctional

Hopelessness

Individual coping, ineffective

Loneliness, risk for

Personal identity disturbance

Powerlessness

Self-esteem, chronic low

Self-esteem, situational low

Self-esteem disturbance

Social interaction, impaired

Social isolation

Spiritual distress

Spiritual well-being, potential for enhanced

7. Psychosocial Well-Being

Problems/Needs

Conflict with staff

Repeated criticism of staff

Unhappiness with roommate

Unhappiness with other residents

Conflict with family

Conflict with friends

Anger with family

Anger with friends

Absence of personal contact with family/friends

Sadness

Lowered self-esteem

Self-accusations

Self-destructive expressions

Feelings of guilt

Feelings of helplessness

Feelings of hopelessness

Feelings of emptiness

Self-centered preoccupation

Mistrust of others

Paranoid feelings

Fear of (specify) _____

Personal identity confusion

Distorted body image

Feelings of euphoria

Grieving

Dysfunctional grieving

Distances self from others

Unease in dealing with others

Unapproachable

Social isolation

Friendless

Feelings of being punished

Bitterness

Inconsolable

Spiritual distress

Ineffective coping

Ineffective family coping

Etiologies

Persistent sad mood

Increasing sad mood

Persistent disturbing behavior

Increasing disturbing behavior

Loss of family member/friend/staff close to resident

Change in room assignment

Loss/change of roommate

Loss of pet/prized possession

Relocation trauma

Use of physical restraints

Delirium

Cognitive decline

Communication deficit

Communication decline

Mobility deficit

Cognitive deficit

Loss/change of status or roles

Unease in dealing with others

Ridicule by others

Unhappiness with nursing home placement

Dependence on others

Chronic debilitation

Inability to provide self-care

Fatigue

Sensory deprivation

Sensory overload

Hearing deficit

Visual deficit

Short-term memory deficit

Separation from loved ones

Change in life-style

Rejection by others

Perceived powerlessness

Feeling of failure

Inability to concentrate

Misdirected anger

Perceived inability to control events

Unrealistic expectations

Adverse reactions from others

7. Psychosocial Well-Being

Goals

The resident will:

Carry on conversation with (name or number of staff persons) _____ by _____

Be critical of staff no more than (number of times) _____ per day by _____

Be noncritical of staff for _____ consecutive days by _____

State happiness with choice of roommate by _____

State happiness with living with roommate by _____

Converse pleasantly with other resident (may specify) by _____

State decrease/elimination of anger toward family/friend by _____

State trust in one person by _____

Carry on conversation about subject other than self by _____

Overtly express anger toward the object that elicits the anger by _____

Identify cause of paranoid feelings by _____

Express that paranoid feelings are inappropriate by _____

Express sadness when situation is sad by _____

Cry in sad situation by _____

Display appropriate affect for situation by _____

Verbalize positive feeling about self by _____

Verbalize positive feeling about body by _____

State all body parts belonging to own body by _____

Recognize body part as own by _____

Smile at _____ by _____

Express control of own fate by _____

Identify at least one self-help measure by _____

Maintain eye contact during a conversation by _____

Initiate eye contact with another by _____

Follow one recommendation without prompting by _____

Express desire for makeup to be applied by _____

Express desire to be clean-shaven by _____

Respond to others without stating guilt feelings by _____

Express desire to live by _____

Base statements in reality by _____

Base behavior in reality by _____

Express concern or interest in welfare of another by _____

Converse with others without swearing or berating by _____

State one positive aspect of environment by _____

State one positive aspect of present situation by _____

Comply with care regime by _____

Verbalize comfort in relationship with (specify) _____ by _____

Make requests of staff politely by _____

Wait own turn for care or assistance from staff by _____

Identify own grieving as dysfunctional by _____

Establish supportive relationship with significant other by _____

Ask for help with coping by _____

Verbalize ability to cope by _____

Request assistance in effective problem solving by _____

Decrease use of ineffective defense mechanisms by _____

Verbalize inability to cope by _____

State feeling of being comfortable living at nursing home by _____

Identify nursing home as "home" by _____

State that stress has improved by _____

Show at least one physical sign that stress is being alleviated by _____

State that the family is experiencing less stress than previously by _____

Share at least one sign from family that they are experiencing decreased stress levels by _____

Allow another to express an opinion on a subject without disagreeing by _____

Work with another in handling own affairs by _____

State acceptance of guardianship by _____

Maintain ability to handle own affairs by _____

Participate in previous religious practices by _____

Participate in religious practices by _____

Verbalize resolution of inner conflict about beliefs by _____

State contentment with current situation by _____

State comfort in conversing with another by _____

Allow another to touch lower arm without moving arm by _____

Interventions

Observe for changes in mental status

Convey acceptance of resident to resident

Provide consistent caregiver

Give repeated honest appraisals of resident's strengths to resident

Talk with resident about unrealistic self-expectations

Approach resident warmly and positively

Respond to suspicious behavior in matter-of-fact and honest manner

Monitor drug levels through test results

Work with physician to adjust medication levels/effects

Introduce resident to other residents on floor

Discuss feelings about placement in nursing home/new room with resident

Provide at least _____ one-to-one session(s) with resident per day

Determine cause of hearing deficit

Monitor/remove wax in ears

Speak in lowered voice pitch

Increase volume of voice without shouting at resident

Touch resident to get resident's attention

Face resident when speaking to resident

Do not cover own mouth when speaking to resident

Do not stand in front of light source when speaking to resident

Encourage loved one(s) to visit/telephone/write resident at least (frequency) _____

Encourage loved one(s) to send tape recording/video recording to resident at least (frequency) _____

Discuss feelings of anger with resident

Discuss options for appropriate channeling of anger with resident

Discuss past successes with resident

7. Psychosocial Well-Being

Interventions, continued

Discuss significant roles still held by resident with resident

Explore possible new roles for resident with resident

Target realistic self-expectations for resident with resident

Place resident in position of almost certain success in an activity

Offer at least one activity to resident in which resident has shown interest

Assist resident in avoiding situations that probably will result in feelings of failure

Provide consistent daily routine for resident

Write down instructions for resident to follow

Have resident repeat instructions

Determine resident's interests

Discuss resident's guilt feelings with resident

Refocus conversation with resident when resident expresses _____

Realistically discuss resident's weakness(es) with resident

Determine options with resident to improve identified weakness(es)

Monitor resident for self-destructive actions

Restrain resident for resident's own protection

Restrain resident for protection of others

Give (specify) _____ medications as ordered

Give explanation to resident if unable to attend to resident immediately

Place resident's wheelchair by nurses' station (frequency, time) _____

Do not argue with resident

Reinforce unacceptability of verbal abuse with resident

Do not discuss possible discharge with resident

Encourage resident to take active social role within facility

Encourage resident to attend at least (number) _____ group activities per _____

Encourage resident to take/continue active social role on unit

Remove resident from public area when resident's language is unacceptable

Talk with resident in calm voice when resident's language is unacceptable

Praise resident for demonstrating desired behavior

Reward resident for demonstrating desired behavior by _____

Place resident in geriatric chair in day room for _____ (time or activity)

Place resident in quiet environment

Provide diversional activities to resident

Consistently approach resident in following manner: _____

Elicit family input for best approach(es) to resident

Monitor behavior changes occurring when new medication is added to regime

Explain procedures before beginning them

Offer opportunity for resident to attend religious services at nursing home

Offer opportunity for resident to attend religious services outside nursing home

Encourage resident to visit with clergy

Encourage discussion of cultural traditions significant to resident

Provide opportunity for resident to follow cultural traditions important to resident, when possible

Discuss beliefs and value systems with resident

Refer to social worker for evaluation and recommendations

Refer to pastoral care for evaluation and recommendations

Encourage resident to visit with pastoral care staff

Call pastoral care staff upon request of _____

Discuss past successful coping mechanisms with resident

Assist resident in selection of appropriate coping mechanisms

Provide emotional support to resident when needed

Assist resident through various phases of grief process

Encourage professional intervention to assist in resolution of dysfunctional grief

Discuss relationship between resident and family with resident/family

Encourage resident to express feelings by _____

Place resident in sensory-integrative activity

Encourage body integration, including body scheme, right–left discrimination, and/or crossing the midline

Allow skills and performance to develop resident's self-concept/self-identity

Refer to occupational therapist for evaluation and recommendations

Assist resident in developing communication skills/ mechanisms

Create a milieu to help resident cope with life's situations

Encourage self-control, including resident's imitating new behavior, being aware of own behavior, and/or directing and redirecting energies into stress-reducing activities and behaviors

Practice problem solving with resident

Implement problem-solving techniques

Offer practice at compromise and negotiation

Offer sensory awareness, including tactile sensation; stereognosis (sense of touch to identify objects); proprioception (position of body in space); ocular control (sight); and/or auditory (hearing), gustatory (taste), and olfactory (smell) awareness

Permit self-expression

Praise self-control

Praise resident when resident talks calmly with another person

Work with resident's significant others in developing alternate coping mechanisms

Allow resident to ventilate feelings regarding
_____

Allow family/significant others to ventilate feelings regarding _____

Introduce family to other residents and staff

Team new resident with resident familiar with facility and floor

Take resident/significant others on tour of facility/unit

Arrange home visit(s)

Encourage parent-child interactions

Offer suggestions for appropriate visiting activities

Encourage development of friendships with other residents

Do not engage resident in discussion of sensitive areas

See resident (frequency) _____ for counseling by _____

See significant others/family (frequency) _____ for counseling by _____

Discuss fear(s) with resident

Discuss implications of not complying with therapeutic regime with resident

Place eyeglasses on resident daily or as needed

Assist resident in maintenance of eyeglasses

Remind resident of maintenance of eyeglasses

Obtain eye exam for resident

Obtain appropriate eyeglasses for resident

Give resident simple tasks to complete

Give one instruction at a time to resident

Talk with resident regarding acceptance of

_____

Use physical restraints only as last alternative

Utilize communication books/device for communication with resident

Teach resident to _____

Instruct family/significant others to _____

Chapter 8

Mod State

Definition

Feelings of sadness, emptiness, anxiety, uneasiness, depression

NANDA-Approved Nursing Diagnoses

Anxiety

Fear

Hopelessness

Individual coping, ineffective

Powerlessness

Self-esteem, chronic low

Self-esteem, situational low

Self-esteem disturbance

Social interaction, impaired

Social isolation

Spiritual distress

Violence, high risk for: Self-directed or directed at others

Problems/Needs

Depression

Sadness

Anxiety

Mental distress

Tearfulness

Sighing

Breathlessness

Motor agitation (for example, pacing, handwringing, picking)

Failure to eat

Failure to take medications

Withdrawal from self-care

Withdrawal from leisure activities

Overriding concern with health

Recurring thoughts of death

Suicidal thoughts

Suicidal actions

Feelings of emptiness

Uneasiness

Limited initiative

No initiative

8. Mood State

Etiologies

Brain deterioration

Brain damage

Drug toxicity

Multiple medications

Medication side effect

Relocation

Dependence on others

Inability to provide self-care

Placement in nursing home

Sensory deprivation

Sensory overload

Hearing deficit

Visual deficit

Sleeplessness

Environmental monotony

Recent loss of close family member/friend

Loss of short-term memory

Separation from loved ones

Change in life-style

Rejection by others

Perceived powerlessness

Feelings of failure

Inability to concentrate

Misdirected anger

Perceived inability to control events

Loss of significant roles

Unrealistic expectations

Restricted physical activity

Adverse reaction from others

Recent change of room assignments

Loss of pet

Loss of loved object

Limited communication ability

Fatigue

Goals

The resident will:

Converse with another without crying by
_____

Decrease number of sighs in _____ (minutes) by
_____

Decrease time spent pacing by _____ (minutes) by
_____

Decrease handwringing time by _____ (minutes) by
_____

Decrease in picking objects off clothing by _____

Eat _____ % of each meal by _____

Eat at least one food by _____

Take medications as prescribed by _____

Express desire for makeup to be applied by _____

Express desire to be clean-shaven by _____

Initiate self-care activity by _____

Complete self-care activity by _____

Participate in at least one group activity by _____

Express concern or interest in welfare of another by
_____

Establish supportive relationship with significant other
by _____

Show at least one physical sign that stress is being
alleviated by _____

State that stress is being alleviated by _____

Follow one recommendation without prompting by _____

Initiate conversation with another by _____

Carry on conversation about subject other than self by _____

Allow/have another person appointed power of attorney for health affairs by _____

Allow/have another person appointed power of attorney for financial affairs by _____

Work with another in handling own affairs by _____

Sit quietly while conversing with another by _____

Express control of own fate by _____

Express desire to live by _____

Interventions

Observe for change in mental status

Encourage verbalization

Convey acceptance of resident to resident

Give repeated honest appraisals of resident's strengths to resident

Talk with resident about unrealistic self-expectations

Provide consistent caregiver

Approach resident warmly and positively

Encourage resident to perform at least _____ activities by self daily

Do not offer assistance for activity before resident attempts activity on own

Introduce resident to other residents on floor

Monitor drug levels through test results for _____

Discuss feelings about placement in nursing home/new room with resident

Keep environmental noises to a minimum

Provide at least _____ one-to-one session(s) with resident per day

Determine cause of hearing deficit

Obtain appropriate hearing device for resident

Place functioning hearing device in resident's ear daily or as needed

Determine cause of visual deficit

Obtain appropriate vision device for resident

Place functioning vision device on resident daily or as needed

Give medication for _____ as ordered

Evaluate effectiveness of medication(s) and side effects

Encourage loved one(s) to visit/telephone/write resident at least (frequency) _____

Encourage loved one(s) to send tape recording/video recording at least (frequency) _____

8. Mood State

Interventions, continued

Praise resident for positive action or statement

Place resident in situation with minimal possibility of rejection by others

Praise resident for completion of activity

Discuss feelings of anger with resident

Discuss options for appropriate channeling of anger with resident

Discuss past successes with resident

Discuss significant roles still held by resident with resident

Explore possible new roles for resident with resident

Target realistic self-expectations for resident with resident

Determine resident's interests

Offer at least one activity to resident in which resident has shown interest

Place resident in area of activity at least (frequency) _____

Place resident in position of almost certain success in an activity

Assist resident to avoid situations that probably will result in feeling of failure

Write down instructions for resident to follow

Discuss resident's guilt feelings with resident

Refocus conversation with resident when resident expresses _____

Realistically discuss resident's weakness(es) with resident

Determine options with resident to improve identified weakness(es)

Monitor resident for self-destructive actions/thoughts

Restrain resident for resident's own protection

Have resident identify at least one positive attribute of self

Refer to _____ for counseling

Refer to _____ for evaluation and recommendations

Acknowledge resident's moods in one-to-one interactions

Place resident by nurses' station (frequency, time) _____

Assist resident back to bed when resident is up at night

Place resident in area where constant observation is possible when the following behavior occurs: _____

Do not argue with resident

Do not discuss possible discharge with resident

Encourage resident to take active social role within facility

Encourage resident to attend at least (number) _____ group activities per _____

Encourage resident to take/continue active social role on unit

Place resident near other residents to encourage interaction

Provide diversional activities to resident

Offer resident simple choices

Praise resident for demonstrating desired behavior

Reward resident for demonstrating desired behavior by _____

Consistently approach resident in following manner: _____

Elicit family input for best approach(es) to resident

Call clergy immediately upon request of resident

Monitor behavior changes/mental status changes/mood state changes when new medication is added

Offer opportunity to attend religious services at/outside long-term care facility

Allow resident to choose sequence for ADL activities

Involve resident in making own schedule of activities

Touch/hug resident to show caring for resident

Emphasize independent actions performed by resident to resident

Transport resident to desired activities

Have resident participate in pet therapy program

Obtain pet for resident that can be kept at nursing home

Obtain pet for resident that can be brought to nursing home for visits

Replace loved object with similar object

Provide resident with communication book/board/device

Teach resident to use communication book/board/device

Discuss past successful coping mechanisms with resident

Assist resident in selection of appropriate coping mechanisms

Provide emotional support to resident/family when needed

Discuss relationship between family and resident with family/resident

Give support to resident regarding _____

Give support to family/significant others regarding

_____

Give family "permission" to visit (frequency)

_____

Allow resident/family/significant others to ventilate feelings regarding _____

Introduce resident/family to other residents and staff

Work with resident to enhance communication skills

Provide distractions for resident when resident discusses

_____

Provide distractions for resident when resident exhibits the following actions/attitudes: _____

Team new resident with resident familiar with facility and floor

Give resident written schedule of activities in facility in which resident may wish to participate

Take resident/family on tour of facility

Arrange home visit(s) for resident

Offer suggestions to resident's significant others for appropriate visiting activities

Encourage resident to develop friendships with other residents

Do not engage resident in discussion of sensitive areas

See family/significant others (frequency) _____ for counseling

Teach resident to _____

Instruct family/significant others to _____

Chapter 9

Behavior Problems

Definition

Problematic manner in which an individual acts

NANDA-Approved Nursing Diagnoses

Self-mutilation, risk for

Sexuality patterns, altered

Violence: self-directed or directed at others, risk for

Problems/Needs

Cries frequently

Agitation

Combative behavior

Anxiety

Rapidly alternating behavior

Verbally abusive behavior

Carelessness with smoking materials

Negative outlook on environment

Consistent refusal of medical treatment

Low frustration tolerance

High level of dependence on others

Eats foreign objects

Passive behavior

Lethargy

Removes clothing in public areas

Demanding behavior

Impatience

Worries frequently

Wanders

Easy distractibility

Inappropriate sexual behavior

Noncompliance to _____

Unresponsive to environmental stimuli (specify) _____

Self-destructive behavior

Self-mutilation

9. Behavior Problems

Etiologies

Alcohol withdrawal

Multiple medications

Medication side effects

Drug toxicity

Cognitive impairment

Separation from loved ones

Change in life-style

Inability to provide self-care

Placement in nursing home

Loss of body function

Knowledge deficit

Loss of short-term memory

Rejection by others

Negative reaction of others

Mistrust of others

Perceived powerlessness

Feeling of failure

Inability to concentrate

Perceived inability to control events

Loss of significant roles

Financial stress

Unrealistic expectations

Restricted physical activity

Misdirected anger

Judgment or reasoning deficit

Misplaced religious beliefs

Anxiety

Fear of failure

Sensory deprivation

Isolation

Separation from religious ties

Separation from cultural ties

Challenged belief/value system

Lack of appropriate opportunity

Lack of appropriate partner

Lack of support system

Value conflict

Spiritual conflict

Skill deficit

Problem-solving skill deficit

Perceived therapeutic ineffectiveness

Perceived invulnerability

Perceived vulnerability

Denial of illness

Situational crisis: (specify) _____

Loss of significant other

Family pattern disruption

Ambivalent family relationships

Unexpressed guilt

Unresolved guilt

Unexpressed anxiety

Unexpressed hostility

Unresolved hostility

Unexpressed despair

Unresolved despair

Terminal illness

Goals

The resident will:

Cry no more than _____ times per
_____ by _____

Sit quietly for 10 minutes upon request by _____

Strike others no more than _____ times per
_____ by _____

Display consistent behavior for (time span)
_____ by _____

Converse with others without swearing or berating by
_____

Use smoking materials safely by _____

State one positive aspect of environment by _____

State one positive aspect of present situation by
_____

Verbalize possible outcome for self as result of refusal of
medical treatment by _____

Accept medical treatment consistently by _____

Accept medical treatment intermittently by _____

Comply with care routine by _____

Comply with medical regime by _____

Initiate at least one self-care activity independently by
_____

Complete at least one self-care activity independently
by _____

Decrease oral intake of foreign objects to no more than
(frequency) _____ per _____
by _____

Eliminate oral intake of foreign objects by _____

Verbalize resolution of inner conflict about beliefs by
_____

Participate in usual religious practices by _____

Return to former religious practices by _____

Verbalize comfort about relationship with deity by
_____

Respond to at least one environmental stimulus by
_____

Participate in at least one complete activity session by
_____

Participate in daily activities by _____

Remain clothed in public area for (time)
_____ by _____

Make requests of staff politely by _____

Wait own turn for care or assistance from staff by
_____

Show decrease in frequency of specific worry by making
fewer statements concerning specific worry by _____

Wander only within specified boundaries by _____

Wander off floor no more than _____ times per
_____ by _____

Complete initiated activity without prompting by
_____

Complete initiated activity by _____

Carry out sexual behavior with self only in privacy of
own room by _____

Identify own grieving as dysfunctional by _____

Sleep at least six hours without interruption per night
by _____

Eat _____ % of meals by _____

Establish supportive relationship with significant other
by _____

Ask for help with coping by _____

Verbalize ability to cope by _____

Request assistance in effective problem solving by
_____

Decrease use of ineffective defense mechanisms by
_____

Maintain appropriate behavioral functioning by
_____

9. Behavior Problems

Goals, continued

Verbalize inability to cope by _____

Budget money to relieve financial stress by _____

Allow/have another person appointed guardian over finances by _____

Give another person power of attorney over _____ by _____

Change payment sources to alleviate financial stress by _____

State acceptance of guardianship/power of attorney by _____

Maintain ability to handle own affairs by _____

Identify cultural ties that bring contentment in nursing home by _____

Identify religious ties that bring contentment in nursing home by _____

Demonstrate understanding of education regarding _____ by _____

Demonstrate no self-destructive behavior by _____

Demonstrate no self-mutilating behavior by _____

Interventions

Place resident in area where constant observation is possible

Do not argue with resident

Reinforce with resident unacceptability of resident's verbal abuse

Instruct resident to ask staff member to light smoking materials

Monitor resident when resident is smoking

Place smoking materials at nurses' station for storage

Give resident limited amount of cigarettes/cigars/pipe tobacco

Remove nonedible but frequently ingested objects from resident's environment

Remove resident from public area when behavior is disruptive

Remove resident from public area when behavior is unacceptable

Talk with resident in calm voice when behavior is disruptive

Praise resident for demonstrating desired behavior

Reward resident for demonstrating desired behavior by _____

Provide diversional activities for resident when _____

Replace removed clothing on resident

Remove resident from public area when resident removes clothing

Dress resident in clothing that is difficult for resident to remove

Encourage resident to verbalize through one-to-one interactions

Consistently approach resident in following manner: _____

Elicit family input for best approach(es) to resident

Call clergy immediately upon request of resident

Monitor behavior changes occurring when new medication is added

Monitor drug levels through test results for

_____

Write out instructions for resident to follow

Have resident repeat instructions

Offer resident opportunity to attend religious services at long-term care facility

Offer resident opportunity to attend religious services outside long-term care facility

Encourage intermittent visits with clergy/pastoral care staff

Encourage discussion of cultural traditions significant to resident

Provide opportunity for resident to follow cultural traditions important to resident, when possible

Ask social worker to discuss finances with resident

Determine with resident ways in which costs can realistically be reduced

Inform resident and/or family of criteria for level of care change

Inform resident and/or family of criteria for financial assistance programs

Assist resident and/or family with financial aid application procedures

Inform resident and/or family of plan for meeting identified criteria

Discuss with resident implications of not complying with therapeutic regime

Provide privacy for sexual activity

Provide private area for interaction with spouse/significant other

Provide uninterrupted time alone with spouse or significant other

Discuss with resident implications of carelessness

Allow denial of illness by resident

Call illness by same term that resident uses

Discuss with resident past successful coping mechanisms

Assist resident in selection of appropriate coping mechanisms

Provide emotional support to resident when needed

Assist resident through various phases of grief process

Discuss relationship between resident and family with resident/family

Encourage resident to express feelings by

_____

Apply restraints when needed for protection of resident/others

Instruct visitors that alcohol may not be brought on the premises

Remove all alcohol from premises

Do not allow resident to leave facility

Place monitoring device on resident that sounds alarms when resident leaves building

Evaluate effectiveness and side effects of medications for possible reduction/discontinuance of some medications

Allow resident to sequence ADL activities provided by staff

Alternate activity with rest periods

Transport resident to activities

Convey acceptance of resident to resident

Provide consistent caregiver

Ensure that staff wear name tags when delivering care to resident

Ensure that staff introduce themselves to resident at initiation of each interaction with resident

Give repeated honest appraisals of resident's strengths to resident

Talk with resident about unrealistic self-view

9. Behavior Problems

Interventions, continued

Approach resident warmly and positively

Do not offer assistance for activity before resident attempts activity on own

Keep environmental noises to a minimum

Approach resident with low, calm voice

Discuss resident's feelings of anger with resident

Discuss resident's options for appropriate channeling of anger with resident

Discuss resident's guilt feelings with resident

Refocus conversation with resident when resident expresses _____

Discuss resident's past success with resident

Discuss with resident significant roles still held by resident

Explore with resident possible new roles for resident

Praise resident for consistent, acceptable behavior

Target with resident realistic self-expectations for resident

Assist resident in avoiding situations that probably will result in feeling of failure

Stimulate memory by _____

Praise resident for finding own room

Label bathroom with picture of toilet

Label bathroom with sign reading "bathroom"

Walk resident to bathroom on request and identify room as bathroom

Give verbal reminders to resident to check activity schedule posted in room before answering questions concerning where resident should go next

Practice problem solving with resident

Teach resident to _____

Instruct family/significant others to _____

Chapter 10

Activities

Definition

Supervised, organized recreation

NANDA-Approved Nursing Diagnoses

Activity intolerance

Activity intolerance, risk for

Diversional activity deficit

Social interaction, impaired

Social isolation

Problems/Needs

No involvement in activities

Little involvement in activities

Apathetic or indifferent to social interaction

Indecisive with regard to any social interaction

Mental inability to participate in activity program

Inappropriate interaction with a group

Diversional activity deficit

Social isolation

Alterations in socialization

Inability to plan own leisure-time activities

Low activity tolerance

Short attention span

Short-term memory deficit

Rejection by others

10. Activities

Etiologies

Cognitive impairment

Fear of (specify) _____

Anxiety (resident unable to define cause)

Chronic debilitation

Low level of consciousness

Impaired thought processes

Low activity tolerance

Apathy

Lethargy

Chronic progressive disease

Frequent lengthy treatments

Impaired mobility

Isolation

Sociocultural dissonance

Distorted body image

Labile emotional behavior

Rude behavior

Inability to empathize with others

Lack of "social graces"

Change in established routine

Translocation syndrome

Mistrust of others

Inability to hear and speak

Emotional conflicts

Problem-solving skills deficit

Situational crisis: (specify) _____

Personal vulnerability

Poor hygienic practices

Activities of interest not offered

Easy fatigability

Environmental barriers

Noisy behavior

Feelings of not belonging to group

Terminal prognosis

Personal choice

Lifelong pattern

Unstable health condition

Schedule conflicts

Frequent naps/sleeping

Goals

The resident will:

Participate in at least _____ activities per _____ by _____

Speak to another when spoken to by _____

Attend at least _____ activities without verbal prompting by _____

State enjoyment of at least one activity after participating in the activity by _____

Show a physical sign of enjoyment following at least one activity by _____

Identify at least two activities that resident would like to participate in by _____

Follow leisure-time activities outlined for resident by _____

Assist with caregivers in outlining leisure-time activities that resident will participate in by _____

Tolerate at least _____ activities per _____ by _____

Attend at least one group activity by _____

Interact appropriately when in a group by _____

Interact appropriately with at least one person by _____

Interact appropriately _____ % of time by _____

Use compensatory mechanisms for memory deficit by _____

Be able to locate bathroom by _____

Be able to find own room by _____

Complete at least _____ activities by _____

Arrive at dining table before meal being served at least _____ % of time by _____

Be able to find dining room without assistance at least _____ % of time by _____

Read time on clock rather than asking what time it is by _____

Show sign of recognizing (person) _____ by _____

State desire to be near a specific person by _____

Open eyes when spoken to by _____

Lie quietly when music is played by _____

Maintain appropriate interaction with others by _____

Maintain appropriate activity participation by _____

Practice appropriate hygienic practices prior to activities by _____

Name at least one activity not currently offered in which the resident would like to participate by _____

Participate in activities that are brief or nonfatiguing by _____

Solicit assistance in getting around environmental barriers preventing participation in activities by _____

Sit quietly throughout activity by _____

State feeling of belonging by _____

Participate in activities appropriate to current health condition by _____

State that nonparticipation in activities is a personal choice by _____

Attend activities/participate in activities as schedule permits by _____

Interventions

Offer opportunities for success and praise as often as possible

Offer schedule of activities for resident to select choice(s)

Initiate conversation with resident as frequently as possible

Evaluate resident's ability to tell time

Give resident opportunity to express opinion of activities attended

Engage resident in group activities

Post identifying pictures outside rooms resident needs to locate (for example, crafts room)

Give resident verbal reminders of activity before commencement of activity

Post personal activity schedule in resident's room

Introduce self to resident before each interaction

Arrange for activity aide to visit and encourage resident to observe specific or designated activity for brief time (frequency) _____

Take resident to one specific assignment or activity (frequency) _____

Establish daily routine with same activity personnel/ volunteers

Familiarize resident with nursing home environment and activity programs on regular basis

Visit (frequency) _____ per day with resident to develop or sustain contact using conversation

Visit (frequency) _____ per day with resident to develop or sustain contact using writing skills

Arrange one-to-one contacts with resident (frequency) _____

Offer ongoing structured activity program for intellectual stimulation

Offer structured activity program directed toward appropriate behavior

10. Activities

Interventions, continued

Offer activity programs directed toward specific interests of resident

Offer activity programs directed toward specific needs of resident

Offer reality orientation on all possible occasions and contacts

Offer positive awareness technique on all possible occasions and contacts

Offer and install visible cues to improve orientation

Provide resident with materials to start and finish projects

Schedule activities to allow for limited energy

Assist resident in planning leisure-time activities

Encourage resident to plan own leisure-time activities

Supervise resident in all activity areas

Encourage activity therapy on individual basis

Play soothing music for (length of time and frequency) _____

Teach resident to _____

Instruct family/significant others to _____

Ensure that resident is clean and is wearing clean clothing for activities

Ensure that resident has brushed teeth prior to going to activity

Transport resident to activities

Place resident in one-to-one activity when resident is noisy

Place resident in appropriate psychosocial group

Provide brief activities for resident

Provide passive activities for resident to enjoy

Remove resident from activity if behavior is unacceptable to others

Respect resident's choice in regard to limited/no activities

Discuss unacceptable behavior with resident

Determine feasibility of offering activities of interest to resident that are not currently offered

Support resident's efforts to overcome situational crisis

Assist resident in getting around environmental barriers

Locate activities on unit on which resident resides

Assist resident in transporting health-related equipment to activities

Chapter 11

Falls

Definition

Coming down suddenly from standing or sitting position

NANDA-Approved Nursing Diagnosis

Injury, risk for

Problems/Needs

Falls

Potential to fall

Multiple falls

Potential for injury

Etiologies

Use of psychotropic drugs

Impaired balance

Poor coordination

Poor leg control

History of falling

Unstable health condition

Unsteady gait

Seizure disorder

Joint pain

Dizziness

Involuntary motor movements

Nonuse or inappropriate use of appliances/devices

Walking without assistance inappropriately

Visual deficit

Responding to bladder/bowel urgency

Environmental factors

Slippery floors

Objects in walkway

Poor illumination

Uneven surfaces

Motor agitation

Inattention to environmental objects

11. Falls

Goals

The resident will:

Receive no injury due to falling by _____

Have no falls by _____

Have decreasing number of falls by _____

Have no more than (number) _____ falls per _____ by _____

Interventions

Ensure that resident wears brace (specify where and when) _____

Apply corset daily

Apply (specify device) _____

Put bedside rails up at night

Put bedside rails up whenever resident is in bed

Put half bedside rails up whenever resident is in bed

Place built-up shoe on resident's foot before ambulating or transferring

Do not leave resident unattended without safety device

Apply (specify type of restraint) _____ when in bed/chair

Give resident verbal reminders not to ambulate or transfer without assistance

Put eyeglasses in place when resident is awake

Store eyeglasses at nurses' station at night

Pad siderails on bed

Put safety bar in place while resident is in wheelchair

Place resident in geriatric chair for (time) _____ per _____

Put additional illumination in resident's bathroom/hallway/room

Use self-releasing safety device when resident is in wheelchair/on stool

Assist resident in walking to activities, dining room, and so forth

Provide walker, cane, quad cane, and so forth for use when ambulating resident

Post signs when floors are wet

Mop floors when residents are not in area

Instruct resident on appropriate use of safety device/appliance

Use wheelchair to transport resident

Evaluate effectiveness and side effects of psychotropic drug(s) for possible decrease in dosage/elimination of drug

Place resident in fall-prevention program

Do not ambulate resident when severe joint pain is present

Establish bladder/bowel regime for resident

Move resident to unit without environmental barriers for this resident

Teach resident to _____

Instruct family/significant others to _____

Rearrange environment to remove barriers for resident

Analyze previous falls by resident to determine whether pattern/trend can be addressed

Chapter 12

Nutritional Status

Definition

State of nourishment

NANDA-Approved Nursing Diagnoses

Nutrition, altered: Less than body requirements

Nutrition, altered: More than body requirements

Nutrition, altered: Potential for more than body requirements

Problems/Needs

Rapid/gradual weight loss

Potential for weight loss

Eats only preferred foods

Excessive snacking between meals

Eats less than _____ % of meals

Decreased appetite

Eats from other residents' trays

Frequently complains of hunger

Underweight

Overweight

Excessive weight gain

Increased requirement for (specify nutrients)
_____

Decreased requirement for (specify nutrients)
_____

Inappropriate intake of (specify nutrients)
_____

Noncompliance with therapeutic diet

12. Nutritional Status

Etiologies

Inability to chew food

Eating many foods with high fat level

Inadequate nutrient intake

Dislike of therapeutic diet

Intolerance of certain foods

Inability to communicate food preferences

Eating salty foods

Inadequate protein intake

Not eating food served

Noncompliance with prescribed diet

Eating food from other residents' trays

Snacking between meals

Knowledge deficit

Perceived inability to digest food

Aversion to eating

Refusal to eat

Reported altered taste sensation

Feeling of fullness after ingesting small amount of food

Sore mouth

Diarrhea

Nausea

Vomiting

Nausea and vomiting

Pain with chewing

Edentulousness

Emotional stress

Social isolation

Food intake/energy expenditure imbalance

Dysfunctional eating patterns

Failure of regulatory mechanisms: (specify)

_____

Taking nutrient-depleting medication: (specify)

_____

Ulcer

Postsurgical requirements

Chronic debilitation

Chronic infection

Translocation syndrome

Postinjury requirements

Eating only preferred foods

Eating inappropriate foods

Unstable health condition

Slowness in self-feeding

Fear that food is poisoned

Fear of gaining weight

Pacing

Anxiety

Depression

Inability to feed self

Swallowing problems

Fear of aspiration

Eating food brought in by family/friends

Goals

The resident will:

Follow restricted diet as ordered by _____

Follow supplemental diet as ordered by _____

Follow therapeutic diet by _____

Have a (specify—for example, iron, blood fat, blood sugar, etc.) _____ blood level within normal range by _____

Have a (specify) _____ urine level within normal range by _____

Have a (specify) _____ blood level within specified range by _____

Have a (specify) _____ urine level within specified range by _____

Lose no more than _____ pounds by _____

Gain at least _____ pounds by _____

Gain no more than _____ pounds by _____

Maintain current weight by _____

Lose at least _____ pounds by _____

Show no signs of protein depletion, such as muscle wasting, by _____

Maintain stable weight by _____

Eat at least one bite of new food by _____

Eat at least one bite of new food each meal for (length of time or number of meals) _____ by _____

Eat no more than _____ foods per _____ not offered on restricted diet by _____

Eat at least one bite of each food served at meal by _____

Eat _____ % of _____ meal(s) by _____

Eat at least _____ % of each food group per _____ by _____

Eat only foods ordered on restricted diet by _____

Not aspirate any food/liquid by _____

Eat food only from own tray by _____

Eat no more than _____ items of food per day from another resident's tray by _____

State feeling of fullness after meal by _____

Not complain of hunger by _____

Complain of hunger no more than _____ times per _____ by _____

Finish each meal by the time all other residents have left dining area by _____

Choke no more than _____ times per _____ by _____

Maintain current eating level by _____

Decrease snacking to _____ times between meals by _____

Eliminate snacking between meals by _____

Eat only food provided by facility by _____

Eat/drink dietary supplement by _____

Eat/drink (amount) dietary supplement (frequency) by _____

12. Nutritional Status

Interventions

Offer foods high in protein

Offer foods high in iron

Do not offer foods high in protein

Praise resident's attempts to follow diet

Provide calculated diabetic diet, including snacks required

Adjust calorie level upward to _____ calories per day

Adjust calorie level downward to _____ calories per day

Allow ample time to ingest meal

Offer between-meal juice _____ times per day

Offer between-meal supplement _____ times per day

Avoid using food as a reward; use other means for positive reinforcement

Evaluate medications that may influence blood sugar levels

Monitor medications that may influence blood sugar levels

Determine food preferences

Ask family/significant others about resident's food preferences

Eliminate concentrated sweets and refined sugars from diet

Eliminate food causing adverse symptoms: (specify)
_____

Prompt resident to eat at least one bite of each food served at meal

Offer high-protein snacks _____ times per day

Offer bedtime snack

Increase portion size at meals

Instruct resident about dietary modifications

Instruct family about dietary modifications for resident

Instruct family about acceptable snacks for resident

Limit snacks and supplements within one hour of mealtime

Do not add salt to foods

Offer foods low in fat

Do not offer fried foods

Offer foods high in potassium

Offer foods low in potassium

Offer fluids every 30 minutes

Limit fluid intake to _____ ml per day

Check blood potassium level (frequency or date)
_____

Check blood sodium level (frequency or date)
_____

Check blood sugar level (frequency or date)
_____

Check blood fat level (frequency or date)
_____

Check hemoglobin level (frequency or date)
_____

Check hematocrit level (frequency or date)
_____

Check blood iron level (frequency or date)
_____

Check ferritin level (frequency or date)
_____

Monitor amount of urine output in 24 hours

Monitor blood pressure (frequency) _____

Determine ideal body weight

Weigh resident every (frequency) _____

Measure height

Monitor weight gain for (time frame)
_____

Monitor weight loss for (time frame)
_____

Check serum protein level (frequency or date)

_____

Monitor dietary regime compliance by resident

Monitor dietary regime compliance by family/significant others

Record food intake for _____ days

Refer to dietitian for evaluation and recommendations

Provide unified positive approach by all staff in support of diet

Maintain present food intake

Offer resident's food preferences

Avoid resident's food dislikes

Evaluate insulin dosage with present caloric intake

Evaluate oral hypoglycemic agent dosage with present caloric intake

Teach resident to _____

Instruct family/significant others to _____

Ask family to limit amount of food brought in to resident

Give food that is easily swallowed to resident

Give food that is easily chewed to resident

Provide ground meat with meals

Hand-feed resident

Use (specify appropriate devices) _____ to assist resident to feed self

Maintain pleasant environment at mealtimes

Offer small feedings _____ times per day

Offer large servings of food

Offer second helpings of food

Offer preferred foods

Offer substitutes for uneaten foods

Ask family to bring preferred foods to resident

Position resident upright for meals

Feed resident slowly

Stimulate swallowing with spoon or by stroking resident's throat

Have suction machine present when resident is eating

Remain with resident during meals

Remove resident from dining area immediately following meals

Place resident at table with other residents' trays out of reach

Assist resident in eating after resident becomes fatigued

Ensure that dentures are in place

Offer clear liquids to resident for (time)

_____

Advance diet as tolerated by resident

Reinforce that resident should eat slowly

Use Heimlich maneuver when needed

Refer to dentist/dental hygienist for evaluation and recommendations

Provide foods/liquids soothing to sore oropharyngeal structures

Eliminate odors from eating area

Provide nondistracting eating environment

Use herbs/spices on foods as allowed by resident's diet

Put incontinent briefs on resident for mealtimes

Ask resident to drink at least _____ glasses of fluid each day

Engage resident in conversation during meal to entice eating as part of socialization

Offer foods high in _____

Offer foods low in _____

Place resident at table with resident's friends

Chapter 13

Feeding Tubes

Definition

Tube to assist resident in maintaining or improving nutritional status

NANDA-Approved Nursing Diagnoses

Aspiration, risk for

Nutrition, altered: Less than body requirements

Oral mucous membrane, altered

Swallowing, impaired

Problems/Needs

Inadequate oral intake

Weight loss

Impaired swallowing

Nutritional deficit

Failure to eat

Resists assistance in eating

Mouth pain

Impaired chewing

Potential for aspiration

Potential for injury

13. Feeding Tubes

Etiologies

Comatose state

Failure to eat

Resists assistance in eating

Swallowing impairment

Chewing problem

Mouth pain

Motor agitation

Depression

Lung aspirations

Muscle paralysis

Muscle weakness

Oral lesion(s)

Loose teeth

Carious teeth

Meal-induced insufficiency of oxygen to blood

Excessive fatigue

Cognitive impairment

Goals

The resident will:

Lose no more than _____ pounds by _____

Lose no more than _____ pounds per _____ by _____

Gain at least _____ pounds by _____

Gain at least _____ pounds per _____ by _____

Maintain current weight by _____

Maintain stable weight by _____

Have oral intake of at least _____ cc per _____ by _____

Eat _____ % of each food group per _____ by _____

Eat _____ % of _____ meal(s) by _____

Aspirate no food/liquid by _____

Accept assistance in eating by _____

Follow verbal cueing for eating by _____

Choke no more than _____ times per _____ by _____

Have no/decreased mouth pain by _____

Swallow food/liquid without difficulty by _____

Eat at least one bite of food by _____

Chew food without difficulty by _____

Have specified intake of (specify nutrient) _____ per _____ by _____

Follow therapeutic diet by _____

Leave feeding tube in place by _____

Interventions

Insert nasogastric tube for feeding purposes

Maintain gastrostomy tube inserted for feeding purposes

Insert _____ tube for feeding purposes

Observe resident for dyspnea

Observe respiratory rate following feeding/eating

Observe for signs of respiratory distress during/following feeding

Give resident small feedings every (frequency) _____

Maintain resident in upright position for (time) _____ after each feeding

Control amount of feeding through gastrostomy tube by use of _____

Give _____ cc of (specify) _____ through gastrostomy tube every (frequency) _____

Use (specify—for example, syringe, pump) _____ for gastrostomy tube feedings

Feed resident orally: (type and amount of liquid/food) _____ every (frequency) _____

Alternate gastrostomy feedings with oral feedings

Feed resident through gastrostomy tube only (time, frequency) _____

Measure residual in stomach before beginning gastrostomy feeding

Plug/clamp tube for (time, frequency, activity, and so forth) _____

Check position of nasogastric tube prior to giving feeding

Check lung sounds prior to/following each feeding

Apply mitt restraints to prevent resident from dislodging feeding tube

Follow therapeutic tube-feeding dietary regime for resident

Remove loose teeth

Remove carious teeth

Change nasogastric tubes every (frequency) _____

Follow therapeutic regime for care of tube-insertion site

Advance oral diet as tolerated

Remove feeding tube when resident can tolerate eating without tube

Medicate for pain prior to eating

Give verbal cues to resident for eating

Monitor intake and output daily

Weigh resident every (frequency) _____

Monitor percent of food eaten by resident from all food groups

Assist resident in eating when resident becomes fatigued

Assure intake of (amount and nutrient) _____ per _____

Keep suction machine in room while feeding resident

Ensure that caregiver has been educated in use of Heimlich maneuver

Teach resident to _____

Instruct family/significant others to _____

Refer resident to dentist

Chapter 14

Dehydration/ Fluid Maintenance

Definition

Fluid output exceeds intake/fluid equilibrium

NANDA-Approved Nursing Diagnoses

Fluid volume deficit

Fluid volume deficit, risk for

Problems/Needs

Fluid volume deficit

Dehydration

Insufficient fluid

Potential for fluid volume deficit

14. Dehydration/Fluid Maintenance

Etiologies

Decreased independent access to fluids

Muted perception of thirst

Diarrhea

Vomiting

Fever

Bleeding

Not consuming all liquids provided

Use of diuretic

Comatose state

Depression

Fluid restriction

Excessive urine output

Frequent use of laxatives

Use of enemas

Excessive sweating

Alcohol abuse

Uncontrolled health conditions

Inability/decreased ability to ask for fluids

Nausea

Cognitive impairment

Refusal to drink liquids

Wound drainage

Satisfying intake with food

Stomach pain

Intestinal pain

Goals

The resident will:

Show decreasing signs of dehydration by _____

Show no signs of dehydration by _____

Attain appropriate fluid volume level by _____

Maintain appropriate fluid volume level by _____

Eliminate cause of fluid volume deficit by _____

Maintain current weight by _____

Lose no more than _____ pounds per _____ by _____

Interventions

Maintain intravenous therapy for hydration purposes

Follow care regime for IV needles, tubing, containers

Offer sips of water (frequency) _____

Offer ice chips (frequency) _____

Give _____ cc of _____ or oral liquids every (frequency) _____

Monitor fluid intake and output daily

Maintain intravenous system for antibiotic delivery to resident

Weigh resident every (frequency) _____

Avoid foods or liquids known to cause (specify symptoms) _____

Record oral intake of resident

Observe resident for signs of pain

Record amount of wound drainage every (frequency) _____

Record amount of bleeding every (frequency) _____

Record frequency, consistency, and amount of emesis

Record frequency and amount of diarrhea

Give (medication) _____ for _____ every (frequency) _____

Keep environmental temperature at _____ degrees

Apply _____ to (location) _____ for _____

Exclude staff members with colds from caring for resident

Ask family/friends not to visit resident if they have communicable diseases

Monitor IV site for swelling, redness, tenderness, and warmth

Discontinue IV at first sign of infiltration/inflammation

Change IV tubing every (frequency) _____

Change IV site every (frequency) _____

Maintain hypodermoclysis for hydration purposes

Monitor hypodermoclysis site for swelling, redness, tenderness, and warmth

Discontinue hypodermoclysis when _____

Change hypodermoclysis site/tubing every _____

Offer oral liquids (amount) _____ every _____

Place straw in glass so resident can drink fluid independently

Provide frequent rest periods for resident

Offer no fluid to resident

Insert indwelling catheter for accurate measurement of urinary output

Monitor effectiveness and side effects of laxatives

Decrease/eliminate use of laxatives for resident

Decrease/eliminate use of enemas for resident

Restrict use of alcohol on premises for resident

Do not allow resident to leave premises

Follow therapeutic regime for care of (condition) _____

Offer liquids before food at meals

Monitor resident for signs of dehydration (tenting skin, dry mouth, and so forth)

Teach resident to _____

Instruct family/significant others to _____

Monitor central line site for redness, swelling, and other signs of infection

Monitor central line for leakage

Flush central line with (amount)_____ of (solution) _____ (frequency) _____

Chapter 15

Dental Care

Definition

Care pertaining to the teeth or oral cavity

NANDA-Approved Nursing Diagnoses

Oral mucous membrane, altered

Pain

Problems/Needs

Broken dentures

Poorly fitting dentures

Edentulousness

Broken partial plate(s)

Poorly fitting partial plate(s)

Oral ulcer

Oral lesion

Oral abscess

Missing teeth

Rash

Loose teeth

Bleeding gums

Gum recession

Swollen gums

Inflamed gums

Mouth pain

Mouth debris

Carious teeth

Malalignment of teeth

15. Dental Care

Etiologies

Improper handling of dentures

Improper storage of dentures

Refusal to wear dentures

Poorly fitting dentures

Broken dentures

Weight loss

Shrinkage of gums

Deterioration of support structure

Poor oral hygiene

Injury

Chronic debilitation

Infection

Carious teeth

Improper tooth brushing

Poorly fitting partial plate(s)

Broken partial plate(s)

Poor diet

Chronic health condition

Unstable health condition

Use of medication that affects gums

Goals

The resident will:

Have dentures repaired by _____

Not break dentures by _____

Not lose dentures by _____

Have properly fitting dentures by _____

Maintain dentures in good repair by _____

Not aspirate tooth by _____

Have loose teeth removed by _____

Maintain unbroken oral mucous membranes by _____

Have oral lesion(s) healed by _____

Be able to chew food sufficiently to swallow by _____

Be able to enunciate words clearly by _____

Be able to eat and drink without pain by _____

Be able to move oral structures without pain by _____

Maintain teeth in good repair by _____

Maintain partial plate(s) in good repair by _____

Obtain new partial plate(s) by _____

Obtain new dentures by _____

Have properly fitting partial plate(s) by _____

Have teeth removed by _____

Arrest gum recession by _____

Have no bleeding of gums by _____

Have decreased bleeding of gums by _____

Have decreased/no swelling of gums by _____

Have decreased/no inflammation of gums by _____

Have no mouth debris by _____

Have no new oral lesions by _____

Have decreased/no bad breath by _____

Provide appropriate oral hygiene for self by _____

Wear dentures by _____

Interventions

Refer to dentist/dental hygienist for evaluation and recommendations

Instruct resident in proper oral hygiene techniques

Instruct resident in proper handling of dentures

Instruct resident in proper storage of dentures

Have dentures realigned

Have resident fitted for new dentures

Prompt resident to put dentures in mouth

Ensure that dentures are labeled

Instruct resident in proper tooth-brushing technique

Monitor oral hygiene provision intermittently

Monitor tooth brushing intermittently

Lay out supplies for tooth brushing

Lay out supplies for denture cleansing

Provide denture care (frequency) _____

Provide oral hygiene (frequency) _____

Place dentures in resident's mouth before meals

Provide food that resident can chew and swallow without difficulty

Apply medication to oral lesion(s) as ordered

Check linen for dentures prior to putting in laundry

Check wastebasket for dentures before emptying

Continue appropriate oral hygiene measures

Continue appropriate denture care

Teach resident to _____

Instruct family/significant others to _____

Follow therapeutic regime that will arrest weight loss

Obtain new dentures for resident

Obtain new partial plate(s) for resident

Instruct resident in placing dentures/partial plate(s) in mouth correctly

Follow therapeutic regime for care of oral injury

Follow therapeutic regime for resolution of infection

Have teeth pulled

Ensure complete repair of carious teeth

Give resident extra oral care while on (medication) _____

Remove resident's dentures before bedtime

Remove dentures for (time) _____ every (frequency) _____

Remove partial plate(s) during night

Remove partial plate(s) for (time) _____ every (frequency) _____

Rinse dentures/partial plate(s) following each meal

Chapter 16

Pressure Ulcers

Definition

Ulceration or interference with structural integrity ranging from upper layer of skin to bone, caused by prolonged pressure in patients who are confined in one position in bed for too long

NANDA-Approved Nursing Diagnoses

Skin integrity, impaired

Skin integrity, risk for impaired

Problems/Needs

Pressure ulcer (stage and description such as size, amount of exudate, etc.) _____

Potential for skin breakdown

Impaired skin integrity

Decubitus ulcer

Bedsore

Etiologies

Nutritional deficit

Chronic debilitation

Immobility

Incontinence

Lack of sensation of body part

Number of risk factors present

Injury

Emaciation

Frequent or constant skin-to-skin contact

Obesity

Friction on skin

Resident positions self in one sitting position only

Resident positions self in one lying position only

Cognitive impairment

Chronic progressive disease

Apathy

Noncompliance with therapeutic regime

Use of trunk, limb, or chair restraints

Constant/frequent perspiration

Inability to respond to painful stimuli

Diminished level of consciousness

Sedation

Frequently sliding down in bed/chair

Agitation

16. Pressure Ulcers

Goals

The resident will:

Follow supplemental diet as ordered by _____

Show reduction of pressure ulcer from stage _____ to stage _____ by _____*

Have reduced/no drainage from pressure ulcer by _____

Have reduced/no foul-smelling drainage from pressure ulcer by _____

Show reduction in size of pressure ulcer by _____

Have no increase in size of pressure ulcer by _____

Have reduction in depth of pressure ulcer by _____

Have reduced/no necrotic tissue in pressure ulcer by _____

Show presence of granulation tissue in pressure ulcer by _____

Show increase of granulation tissue in pressure ulcer by _____

Have no increase in number of pressure ulcers by _____

Show reduction in number of pressure ulcers by _____

Show no signs of infection in or around pressure ulcer by _____

Have a decrease in number of risk factors for skin breakdown present by _____

Allow positioning in _____ number of sitting positions by _____

Allow positioning in _____ number of lying positions by _____

Comply with therapeutic regime by _____

Maintain intact skin integrity by _____

_____
*Reduction of pressure sores from one stage to another is viewed differently by some researchers and regulatory agencies. Therefore, this goal is included as an option for selection.

Interventions

Reassess pressure ulcers at least weekly

Perform abbreviated nutritional assessment at least every three months

Offer supplemental nutrition to resident every _____ hours

Record amount of supplemental diet consumed daily

Record percentage of meals eaten daily

Give (measurement) _____ of _____ for supplemental nutrition (frequency) _____

Assess for pain related to pressure ulcer or its treatment

Manage pressure ulcer/treatment pain by (specify) (eg— covering wounds, repositioning, adjusting support surfaces) _____

Follow house protocol/regime for treating breaks in skin integrity/pressure ulcers

Perform following routine: (specify) _____ (frequency) _____ for skin breakdown of _____

Give (medication) _____ every _____ for _____

Place insulated ice on area of skin integrity break: (specify) _____ for _____

Place warm, moist cloth on _____ for _____

Have _____ people move resident to avoid skin friction rubs

Use turn sheet to turn resident to avoid shearing forces on skin

Cleanse perineal area with soap and water following each urination

Cleanse perineal area with soap and water following each bowel movement

Cover (area of skin break) _____ with _____ (frequency) _____

Cleanse wound (specify area) _____ with _____ (frequency) _____

Use _____ to assist resident in maintaining position

Lubricate skin with _____ (frequency) _____

Encourage resident to carry out regime or portions of regime on own

Ensure that staff members take initiative in carrying out regime with resident

Insert indwelling catheter until skin breakdown heals

Turn and position resident every _____ hours as indicated by individual turning schedule

Reposition resident every (frequency) _____

Teach resident risk factors for development of pressure ulcers

Teach family/significant others risk factors for development of pressure ulcers

Check (body part) _____ with lack of sensation for skin breaks

Walk resident _____ feet (frequency) _____ with assistance of _____

Take resident to stool/commode every (frequency) _____

Put resident on bedpan every (frequency) _____

Correct cause of previous injury to prevent reoccurrence

Place _____ between area of skin-to-skin contact (specify area) _____

Teach resident to _____

Instruct family/significant others to _____

Place resident in skin-breakdown–prevention program

Try alternate measures before using restraints with resident

Walk resident (distance) _____ every (frequency) _____

Instruct resident/family on consequences of non-compliance with therapeutic regime

Pad side bedrails to prevent injury to resident

Place pressure-relieving product (specify)_____ on bed/chair/other

Place foam mattress on bed/chair for comfort

Place static air mattress on bed/chair

Place alternating/dynamic air mattress on bed/chair

Place gel mattress/pad on bed/chair

Place water mattress on bed

Place resident on low-air-loss bed

Place resident on air-fluidized bed

Remove adult incontinence brief when resident is on low-air-loss bed

Remove adult incontinence brief when resident is on air-fluidized bed

Place resident in whirlpool (frequency) _____ for (length of time) _____

Chapter 17

Psychotropic Drug Use

Definition

Drug having an altering effect on the mind

NANDA-Approved Nursing Diagnoses

Activity intolerance, risk for

Aspiration, risk for

Communication, impaired verbal

Confusion, acute

Constipation

Environmental interpretation syndrome, impaired

Hopelessness

Powerlessness

Injury, risk for

Oral mucous membrane, altered

Physical mobility, impaired

Self-care deficit

Swallowing, impaired

Thought processes, altered

Tissue perfusion, altered

Urinary elimination, altered

Urinary retention

Violence: self-directed or directed at others, risk for

Problems/Needs

Falls

Hypotension

Dizziness

Syncope

Loss of voluntary extremity movement

Unsteady gait

Loss of ability to position

Loss of ability to turn body while standing

Motor agitation

Involuntary movements of mouth, face, and so forth

Poor balance

Muscular rigidity

Tremors

Marked decrease in spontaneous movements

Delirium

Withdrawal

Depression

Hallucinations

Delusions

Decline in ADL self-performance

Deterioration in intellectual function

Deterioration in communication

17. Psychotropic Drug Use

Problems/Needs, continued

Deterioration in mood

Deterioration in behavior

Incontinence

Constipation

Fecal impactions

Urinary retention

Dry mouth

Impaired communication

Potential for drug toxicity

Potential for injury

Potential for aspiration

Etiologies

Hypotension

Dizziness

Syncope

Loss of voluntary movement

Unsteady gait

Poor balance

Loss of ability to position

Motor agitation

Medication side effects

Drug toxicity

Medication interactions

High/low dosage of medication

Noncompliance with medication(s)

Difficulty swallowing

Difficulty chewing

Goals

The resident will:

Show minimal/no side effects of medications taken by
_____

Have drug (name) _____ blood level within therapeutic range by _____

Have drug (name) _____ blood level within specified range by _____

Have no injury related to medication usage/side effects by _____

Take medication(s) as ordered by _____

Not show (specify) _____ as side effect of medication use by _____

Show decreased/no involuntary extremity movement by
_____

Show declined/no motor agitation by _____

Show no involuntary movements of mouth, face, and so forth by _____

Show no muscular rigidity in walking by _____

Have no/decreased number of falls by _____

Interact appropriately with others by _____

Show no signs of hallucinating by _____

Have no delusional thinking by _____

Perform own ADLs by _____

Have regular bowel elimination pattern by _____

Show decreased/no constipation by _____

Have no fecal impactions by _____

Have regular urinary elimination pattern by _____

Follow continence program by _____

Have no/reduced number of urinary incontinence by
_____

Show improvement in mood by _____

Show improvement in behavior by _____

Show improved reasoning capacity by _____

Show no signs of tremors by _____

Communicate appropriately with others by _____

Demonstrate steady gait by _____

Show no signs of aspiration by _____

Have a reduction in number of medications requested by _____

Show progress toward normal/therapeutic blood drug range of _____ by _____

Maintain normal/therapeutic blood drug range of
_____ by _____

17. Psychotropic Drug Use

Interventions

Evaluate effectiveness and side effects of medications for possible decrease/elimination of psychotropic drugs

Evaluate effectiveness and side effects of medications for possible need to increase psychotropic drugs

Monitor pharmacist's drug regime review for identification of potential drug interactions

Change frequency of (specify) _____ from _____ to _____ and monitor for effectiveness and side effects

Monitor drug blood levels for (specify) _____ every _____

Take and record pulse/respiration/blood pressure prior to giving medication

Discuss side effects of drugs with resident

Take blood pressure in sitting position and then in standing position every (frequency) _____

Take blood pressure in lying position and then in sitting position every (frequency) _____

Use wheelchair for transportation when resident _____

Provide safety device to maintain position while resident is sitting

Decrease dosage of psychotropic drugs until signs of tardive dyskinesia disappear

Monitor interaction of resident with others for appropriateness

Give resident opportunity to perform portions (specify) _____ of own ADLs

Monitor resident's bowel elimination pattern

Follow resident's bowel regime for establishing elimination routine

Check resident for fecal impactions every (frequency) _____

Monitor resident's mood state

Monitor resident's behavior in public/in private

Offer resident opportunities to problem solve (reasoning)

Monitor resident for signs of tremor

Observe resident's gait for steadiness, balance, muscle coordination, ability to position and turn

Use walker/other device to assist resident in walking

Do not allow resident to walk without assistance of staff

Monitor resident's mental status functioning on ongoing basis

Monitor resident's incontinence—frequency, amount, timing, and so forth

Teach resident to _____

Instruct family/significant others to _____

Chapter 18

Physical Restraints

Definition

Application or use of an external device for prevention of injury to oneself or to someone else

NANDA-Approved Nursing Diagnoses

Disuse syndrome, risk for

Impaired skin integrity, risk for

Injury, risk for

Physical mobility, impaired

Tissue perfusion, altered

Violence, risk for: Self-directed or directed at others

Problems/Needs

Impaired balance

Falls

Impaired mobility

Actual/potential for self-directed violence

Actual/potential for violence directed at others

Muscle weakness

Potential local circulatory deficit

Limb edema

Potential for seizures

Potential for injury

Bedfast

Removal of device (specify) (e.g., catheter, G-tube, IV, other)

Impaired wound healing

Impaired postsurgical wound healing

Noncompliance with wound care therapeutic regime

Noncompliance with postsurgical therapeutic regime

18. Physical Restraints

Etiologies

Lack of sensation of body part

Misdirected anger

Loss of balance

Consistent leaning position

Injury

Unstable health condition

Seizures

Lethargy

Alcohol withdrawal

Cognitive impairment

Decreased strength

Decreased local circulation

Anger

Unrealistic expectations

Hallucinations

Delusions

Dependent position of extremity

Motor agitation

Postsurgery therapeutic regime

Wound care regime

Delirium

Anxiety

Resistance to treatment/medications/nourishment

Psychotropic drug side effects

Goals

The resident will:

Not injure self by _____

Not injure another by _____

Not hit caregiver or other person by _____

Maintain current muscle strength by _____

Show intact muscle integrity by _____

Tolerate (activity) _____ by _____

Tolerate (activity) _____ times per _____ by _____

Maintain current circulatory status in (location) _____ by _____

Show signs of improved circulatory status in (location) _____ by _____

Not fall by _____

Have no more than _____ falls per _____ by _____

Not injure self in fall by _____

Not injure self during seizure by _____

Maintain upright position by _____

Show decreased/no limb edema by _____

Have strong pulses in area distal to restraint by _____

Maintain ability to walk when not using physical restraints by _____

Cooperate with wound care regime by _____

Cooperate with postsurgery therapeutic regime by _____

Interventions

Monitor fingers daily for color, warmth, and sensation when mitt restraints are used

Monitor skin daily for signs of pressure areas

Apply restraint (specify type) _____ when _____

Pad side rails on bed

Use safety device (specify) _____ when _____

Place resident in geriatric chair when _____

Have resident use wheelchair when _____

Have resident use walker when _____

Place resident in restraint-reduction program

Try alternative devices before using physical restraints with resident

Use least restrictive device feasible (specify) _____

Monitor limb distal to restraint for color, warmth, sensation, pulses every (frequency) _____

Discuss unacceptable behavior by resident with resident

Monitor muscle strengthening exercises

Walk resident (distance) _____ every (frequency) _____

Remove restraint every _____ for _____

Discuss necessity of restraining device for resident with resident/family

Monitor number/seriousness of falls for resident

Place resident in fall-prevention program

Give (medication) _____ as ordered for _____

Measure limb circumference every _____

Follow wound care regime as ordered

Follow postsurgery therapeutic regime as ordered

Teach resident to _____

Instruct family/significant others to _____

Appendix

NANDA-Approved Nursing Diagnoses

Activity intolerance

Activity intolerance, risk for

Adaptive capacity: intracranial, decreased

Adjustment, impaired

Airway clearance, ineffective

Anxiety

Aspiration, risk for

Body image disturbance

Body temperature, risk for altered

Breastfeeding, effective

Breastfeeding, ineffective

Breastfeeding, interrupted

Breathing pattern, ineffective

Caregiver role strain

Caregiver role strain, risk for

Communication, impaired verbal

Community coping, ineffective

Community coping, potential for enhanced

Confusion, acute

Confusion, chronic

Constipation

Constipation, colonic

Constipation, perceived

Decisional conflict (specify)

Decreased cardiac output

Defensive coping

Denial, ineffective

Diarrhea

Disuse syndrome, risk for

Diversional activity deficit

Dysfunctional ventilatory weaning response (DVWR)

Dysreflexia

Energy field disturbance

Environmental interpretation syndrome, impaired

Family coping, compromised, ineffective

Family coping, disabling, ineffective

Family coping: potential for growth

Family processes, altered

Family processes: alcoholism, altered

Fatigue

Fear

Fluid volume deficit

Fluid volume deficit, risk for

Fluid volume excess

Gas exchange, impaired

Grieving, anticipatory

Appendix

Grieving, dysfunctional

Growth and development, altered

Health maintenance, altered

Health-seeking behaviors (specify)

Home maintenance management, impaired

Hopelessness

Hyperthermia

Hypothermia

Incontinence, bowel

Incontinence, functional

Incontinence, reflex

Incontinence, stress

Incontinence, total

Incontinence, urge

Individual coping, ineffective

Infant behavior, disorganized

Infant behavior, potential for enhanced organized

Infant behavior, risk for disorganized

Infant feeding pattern, ineffective

Infection, risk for

Injury, risk for

Knowledge deficit (specify)

Loneliness, risk for

Management of therapeutic regimen: community, ineffective

Management of therapeutic regimen: families, ineffective

Management of therapeutic regimen: individual, ineffective

Management of therapeutic regimen, ineffective

Memory, impaired

Noncompliance (specify)

Nutrition: less than body requirements, altered

Nutrition: more than body requirements, altered

Nutrition: potential for more than body requirements, altered

Oral mucous membrane, altered

Pain

Pain, chronic

Parental role conflict

Parent/infant/child attachment, risk for altered parenting

Parenting, altered

Parenting, risk for altered

Parenting, high risk for altered

Perioperative positioning injury, risk for

Peripheral neurovascular dysfunction, risk for

Personal identity disturbance

Physical mobility, impaired

Poisoning, risk for

Post-trauma response

Powerlessness

Protection, altered

Rape-trauma syndrome

Rape-trauma syndrome: Compound reaction

Rape-trauma syndrome: Silent reaction

Relocation stress syndrome

Role performance, altered

Self-care deficit, bathing/hygiene

Self-care deficit, feeding

Self-care deficit, dressing/grooming

Self-care deficit, toileting

Self-esteem, chronic low

Self-esteem disturbance

Self-esteem, situational low

Self-mutilation, risk for

Sensory/perceptual alterations (specify) (visual, auditory, kinesthetic, gustatory, tactile, olfactory)

Sexual dysfunction

Sexuality patterns, altered

Skin integrity, altered

Skin integrity, risk for impaired

Sleep pattern disturbance

Social interaction, impaired

Social isolation

Spiritual distress (distress of the human spirit)

Spiritual well-being, potential for enhanced

Suffocation, risk for

Sustain spontaneous ventilation, inability to

Swallowing, impaired

Thermoregulation, ineffective

Thought processes, altered

Tissue integrity, impaired

Tissue perfusion, altered (specify type) (renal, cerebral, cardiopulmonary, gastrointestinal, peripheral)

Trauma, risk for

Unilateral neglect

Urinary elimination, altered

Urinary retention

Violence: self-directed or directed at others, risk for

Source: *Classification of Nursing Diagnoses — Proceedings of the Eleventh Conference, North American Nursing Diagnosis Association (NANDA).* Glendale, CA: CINAHL Information Systems, 1994.

Index

Abdominal pressure, 29, 36
Activities, 59–62
    deficits in, 59
    diversional, 95
    low tolerance of, 60
    risk for intolerance in, 59, 87, 95
Activities of daily living
    decline in self-performance of, 8, 87
    functional/rehabilitation potential
        bathing, 33–34, 96
        dressing, 24–26, 96
        eating, 27–28, 96
        mobility, 19–23, 96
        personal hygiene, 31–32, 96
        toileting, 29–30, 96
Adaptive capacity, decreased intracranial, 7, 95
Adjustment, impaired, 39, 95
ADL. *See* Activities of daily living
Adverse reactions, 41, 48
Agitation, 53, 83
Airway clearance, 95
Alcohol abuse, 76
Alcohol withdrawal, 54, 92
Allergies
    to food, 27
    to soap, 33
Ambivalent family relationships, 54
Anal sore, 29
Anger, 27, 40, 41, 48, 54, 92
Anxiety, 1, 2, 20, 29, 36, 39, 47, 53, 54, 60, 66, 92, 95
Apathy, 59, 60, 83
Aphasia, 36
    expressive, 15
    receptive, 15
Appearance
    inability to maintain, 31
    lack of interest in, 31
Appetite, decreased, 65
Appliances/devices, nonuse of, 63
Arm mobility, impaired, 20, 27

Arm strength
    decreased, 20, 29
    impaired, 27
Aspiration
    fear of, 66
    of food, 27
    lung, 72
    risk for, 71, 87, 88, 95
Assessment, in long-term care plan, vii
Atrophic vaginitis, 36
Attention span, poor, 31, 59
Aversion to eating, 66

Balance
    loss of, 92
    poor, 20, 29, 63, 87, 88, 91
Bathing, problems with, 31–32
Bed
    immobility in, 19
    positioning in, 83
Bedfastness, 19, 91
Bedsores, 83
Behavior
    combative, 53
    demanding, 53
    disturbing, 41
    health-seeking, 96
    inappropriate sexual, 53
    infant, 96
    labile emotional, 60
    noisy, 60
    problems with, 53–58, 88
    rapidly alternating, 53
    self-destructive, 40, 53
    verbally abusive, 53
    worsening, 1
Belief/value system, challenged, 54
Belonging, feelings of, 60
Bitterness, 40
Bladder
    inability to empty, 36

    loss of muscle tone, 36
    responding to feelings of urgency, 2, 63
    spasms of, 36
Bleeding, 76
    of gums, 79
Blindness, 11
Blood calcium level, 36
Blood pressure, drop in, 20
Blood sugar level, 2, 8, 36
Blurry vision, 11
Body, loss of ability to turn, 87
Body function, loss of, 54
Body image disturbance, 39, 40, 60, 95
Body part
    inability to move, 19
    lack of sensation of, 20, 83, 92
Body temperature, risk for altered, 95
Bowel elimination, ineffective, 29
Bowel pressure, 29
Bowel urgency, 2, 63
Brain damage, 8, 48
Brain deterioration, 8, 48
Breastfeeding, 95
Breathing pattern, 95
Breathlessness, 47

Cardiac function, inadequate, 2, 8
Cardiac output, decreased, 95
Casting of joints, 20
Cataracts, 11
Cathartic, 29
Catheter manipulation, 36
Central vision, impaired, 11
Chair, positioning in, 83
Chewing, impaired, 27, 66, 71, 72, 88
Choking, 27
Circulation
    decreased local, 92
    inadequate, 2
    potential deficit in, 91
Clinical condition, lack of control of, 36

Index

Clothing
  inability to fasten, 24
  inability to take off/put on, 24
  inappropriate choices in, 24
  inappropriate removal of, 24, 53
Cognitive deficit, 31, 41
Cognitive impairment, 16, 20, 27, 29, 33,
    36, 41, 54, 60, 72, 76, 83, 92
Cognitive loss, 7–10
Colostomy, 29
Comatose state, 36, 72, 76
Combative behavior, 53
Communication, 15–17
  deterioration in, 41, 87
  impaired verbal, 1, 7, 15, 35, 76, 87, 88
  limited ability in, 48, 66
  misunderstanding of, 7
Concentration, inabilities in, 41, 48, 54
Conflict, 40
  decisional, 39
Confusion
  acute, 1, 87, 95
  chronic, 7, 95
Consciousness, level of, 60, 83
Constipation, 8, 29, 87, 88, 95
Continence, decline in, 8
Coordination
  poor, 19, 31, 63
  problems in, 20
Coping
  defensive, 39
  ineffective, 40, 47, 95, 96
Crying, 53
Cultural ties, separation from, 54

Death. See also Loss
  recurring thoughts of, 47
Debilitation
  chronic, 41, 60, 66, 83
  general, 20, 29
Decision-making, difficulty in, 7, 95
Decubitus ulcer, 83
Defensive coping, 95
Dehydration, 2, 75–77
Delirium, 1–6, 36, 41, 87, 92
Delusions, 1, 87, 92
Demanding behavior, 53
Dementia, 7–10
Denial, ineffective, 39, 95
Dental care, 79–81
Dentures
  broken, 80
  improper handling of, 80
  poorly fitting, 80
  problems with, 27, 79
  refusal to wear, 80
Dependency, 41, 48, 53

Depression, 2, 20, 36, 47, 66, 72, 76, 87
Despair, unexpressed/unresolved, 54
Device removal, 91
Diarrhea, 29, 66, 76, 95
Diet. See also Eating; Nutrition
  noncompliance with, 65, 66
  poor, 80
Disease, chronic progressive, 60
Disorientation, 1, 7
Distractibility, 1, 53
Disturbing behavior, 41
Disuse syndrome, risk for, 19, 91, 95
Diuretics, 36, 76
Diversional activity deficit, 59
Dizziness, 63, 87, 88
Double vision, 11
Dressing, problems with, 24–26
Drug toxicity, 2, 48, 54, 88
Dysfunctional ventilatory weaning response, 95
Dysreflexia, 95

Ear infection, 16
Earwax accumulation, 16
Eating. See also Diet; Nutrition
  dysfunctional patterns in, 66
  foreign objects, 53
  problems with, 27–28, 47, 72
  resistance to assistance in, 72
Eating utensils, inability to use, 27
Edema
  joint, 20
  limb, 20, 91
  pedal, 36
Edentulousness, 27, 66, 79
Emaciation, 83
Emotional conflicts, 60
Emotional stress, 66
Empathy, inability in, 60
Emptiness, feelings of, 40, 47
Energy field disturbance, 95
Environment
  barriers in, 20, 36, 60
  changing awareness of, 1
  factors in, 63
  inattention to objects in, 63
  negative outlook on, 53
  unresponsiveness to stimuli in, 2, 7, 53
Environmental interpretation syndrome,
    impaired, 7, 87, 95
Environmental monotony, 48
Euphoria, feelings of, 40
Evaluation, in long-term care plan, x
Events, perceived inabilities to control, 41,
    48, 54
Expectations, unrealistic, 41, 48, 54, 92
Extremities
  decreased strength in, 20, 29

dependent position of, 92
impaired mobility of, 20, 27, 29
impaired strength of, 27
loss of sensation in, 29
loss of voluntary movement of, 87
problems with controlling, 20
Eye
  medications for, 11
  pain in, 11
  removal of, 11
Eyeglasses
  broken, 11
  ill-fitting, 11
  lack of, 11
  nonuse, 11

Failure
  to eat, 72
  feelings of, 41, 48, 54
Falls, 63–64, 87, 91
Family member
  conflict with, 40
  reaction to loss of, 2, 41, 48
Family pattern disruption, 54
Family processes, altered, 95
Family relationships, ambivalent, 54
Fantasizing episodes, 2
Fatigue, 20, 27, 29, 31, 41, 48, 60, 72, 95
Fear, 33, 36, 39, 40, 47, 60, 66, 95
Fecal impaction, 2, 8, 29, 36, 88
Feeding tubes, 71–73
Fever, 2, 76
Financial stress, 54
Fluids
  access to, 76
  excessive intake of, 36
  inability to ask for, 76
  inability to drink, 76
  inadequate intake of, 36
  maintenance of, 75–77
  restrictions on, 76
Fluid volume deficit, 75, 95
Fluid volume excess, 95
Food
  allergies to, 27
  choice, 66
  dislikes, 27
  inability to chew, 66
  intolerances of, 66
Food intake/energy expenditure imbalance,
    66
Foreign objects, eating of, 53
Friendlessness, 40
Friends
  conflict with, 40
  reaction to loss of, 2, 41, 48
Frustration, low tolerance of, 53

Gait, unsteady, 63, 87, 88
Gas exchange, impaired, 95
Goals, components of, ix
Goal statements, ix
Grieving, 40, 95
    dysfunctional, 39, 96
Group interaction, inappropriate, 59
Growth and development, altered, 96
Guilt
    feelings of, 40
    unexpressed/unresolved, 54
Gums
    bleeding, 79
    inflamed, 79
    recession, 79
    shrinkage of, 80

Hair
    inability to comb/brush, 31
    inability to shampoo, 31
Hallucinations, 1, 87, 92
Hand mobility, impaired, 27
Hand strength, impaired, 27
Head trauma, 2, 11
Health condition
    chronic, 80
    uncontrolled, 76
    unstable, 20, 60, 63, 80, 92
Health maintenance, altered, 96
Health-seeking behaviors, 96
Hearing
    decreased, 15
    deficit in, 2, 16, 41, 48
    inabilities in, 60
    loss of, 8
Hearing aid, nonuse of, 16
Helplessness, feelings of, 40
Hemorrhoids, 29
Home maintenance management, 96
Hopelessness, 39, 40, 47, 87, 96
Hostility, unexpressed/unresolved, 54
Hyperthermia, 96
Hypnotics, 36
Hypotension, 87, 88
Hypothermia, 96

Illness
    denial of, 54
    recovering from, 20
Illumination, poor, 63
Immobility, 36, 83
Impatience, 53
Implementation, in long-term care plan, x
Inconsolability, 40
Incontinence, 35–38, 83, 88, 96
Indeciveness, 59

Infant behavior, 96
Infections, 2, 8, 11, 16, 29, 36
    chronic, 66
    ear, 16
    risk for, 35, 96
    urinary tract, 35
Information, dereriorating ability to com-
    municate, 1
Initiative, limited, 47
Injuries, 80, 83, 92
    potential for, 19, 35, 71, 88, 91
    risk for, 7, 63, 87, 91, 96
Intellectual function, deterioration in, 1, 87
Interpersonal activities, decreased interest
    in, 2
Intestinal pain, 76
Invulnerability, perceived, 54
Isolation, 2, 54, 60

Joints
    casting of, 20
    contracture, 19
    edema, 20
    impaired movements of, 20
    pain in, 63
    splinting of, 20
Judgment deficit, 7, 54

Knowledge deficit, 20, 54, 66, 96

Labile emotional behavior, 60
Laxatives, 29, 76
Leaning, 19, 92
Leg control, poor, 63
Leisure activities
    inability to plan own, 59
    withdrawal from, 1, 47
Lens prescription, incorrect, 11
Lethargy, 1, 20, 29, 31, 53, 60, 92
Lifelong pattern, 60
Life-style changes, 2, 41, 48, 54
Limb edema, 91
Loneliness, 39, 96
Long-term care manual, xi–xv
Long-term care plan
    case study and sample, xvi–xviii
    components of, viii–x
Loss(es)
    of pet, 41, 48
    reaction to, 2
    reaction to, for family member/friend,
        2, 41, 48
Loved object, loss of, 48
Loved ones, separation from, 2, 41, 48, 54
Lung aspiration, 72

Makeup, inability to apply, 31
Meal-induced insufficiency of oxygen to
        blood, 72
Measurable goals, ix
Medical treatment, refusal of, 53
Medications, 29
    affecting gums, 80
    diuretics, 36, 76
    dosage level of, 88
    eye, 11
    failure to take, 47
    hypnotics, 36
    interactions, 2, 8, 88
    multiple, 2, 48, 54
    noncompliance with, 88
    nutrient-depleting, 66
    psychotropic, 63, 87–90
    resistance to, 92
    sedatives, 20, 36
    side effects from, 2, 8, 11, 16, 48, 54,
        88, 92
    tranquilizing, 20
Memory deficit, 7, 96
    long-term, 7
    short-term, 7, 31, 33, 36, 41, 48, 54, 59
Mental distress, 47
Mental function, impaired, 1
Mental illness, 8
Mental retardation, 8
Minimum data set (MDS), viii
Mistrust of others, 40, 54, 60
Mobility
    deficit, 19–23, 41, 91
    impaired, 33, 36, 60
Mood
    deterioration in, 88
    disorders in, 8
    problems, 2
Mood state, 47–51
Motor agitation, 1, 47, 63, 72, 87, 88, 92
Motor movements, involuntary, 63
Motor responses, inappropriate, 7
Mouth
    debris, 79
    dry, 88
    pain in, 71, 72, 79
    sores in, 27, 66
Movement
    decrease in spontaneous, 87
    imposed restrictions of, 19
    involuntary, 31, 87
    loss of voluntary, 88
    problems with independent, 20
Muscle movements, involuntary, 31, 87
Muscle paralysis, 16, 27, 72
Muscle weakness, 16, 20, 27, 31,
        72, 91
Muscular rigidity, 87

Index

Nausea, 27, 66, 76
Negative reactions, 54
Neglect, unilateral, 97
Noisy behavior, 60
Noncompliance, 53, 96
Nursing home placement, 41, 48, 54
Nutrition. *See also* Diet; Eating
   altered, 65, 71, 96
   resistance to, 92
Nutritional deficit, 71, 83
Nutritional status, 65–69

Obesity, 83
Omnibus Budget Reconciliation Act (1987),
   viii
Opportunity, lack of appropriate, 54
Oral abscess, 79
Oral hygiene, poor, 80
Oral intake, inadequate, 71
Oral lesions, 72
Oral mucous membrane, altered, 71, 79, 87,
   96
Oral ulcers, 79
Overweight, 65

Pacing, 66
Pain, 8, 20, 29, 66, 96
   intestinal, 76
   joint, 63
   mouth, 71, 72, 79
   related to urination, 35, 36
   stomach, 76
Paranoid feelings, 40
Parental role conflict, 96
Parent/infant/child attachment, 96
Parenting, altered, 96
Partner, lack of appropriate, 54
Pedal edema, 36
Peripheral enurovascular dysfunction, risk
   for, 19, 96
Person, disorientation to, 1, 7
Personal activities, decreased interest in, 2
Personal choice, 60
Personal contact, absence of, 40
Personal hygiene, problems with, 31–32, 60
Personal identity disturbance, 39, 40, 96
Personal vulnerability, 60
Perspiration, 83
Pet, loss of, 41, 48
Physical activity, restricted, 48, 54
Physical mobility, impaired, 1, 19, 87, 91,
   96
Physical restraints, 2, 8, 20, 36, 41, 83,
   91–93
Place, disorientation to, 1, 7
Planning, in long-term care plan, viii–x

Planning interventions, x
Poisoning, risk for, 96
Positioning, problems in, 20, 83, 87, 88
Postinjury requirements, 66
Postsurgical requirements, 66
Postsurgical therapeutic regime, noncompli-
   ance with, 91, 92
Post-trauma response, 96
Powerlessness, perceived, 39, 48, 54, 87, 96,
   941
Pressure ulcers, 83–85
Problem behavior, worsening, 1
Problem/need statements, viii–x
Problem-solving skill deficit, 54, 60
Pronounciation, problems with, 15
Protection, altered, 96
Protein intake, inadequate, 66
Psychiatric disorder, 16
Psychosocial distress, 2
Psychosocial well-being, 39–45
Psychotropic drugs, 63, 87–90
   side effects from, 92
Punishment, feelings of, 40
Pupil, changes in size of, 11

Range of motion, limited, 19, 20
Rape-trauma syndrome, 96
Rapidly alternating behavior, 53
Rash, 79
Reassessment, in long-term care plan, x
Rectal fissure sore, 29
Redicule by others, 41
Regulatory mechanisms, failure of, 66
Rejection, 41, 48, 54, 59
Religious beliefs, misplaced, 54
Religious ties, separation from, 54
Relocation stress syndrome, 1, 96
Relocation trauma, 2, 41, 48
Resident Assessment Protocols (RAPs), viii
Respiratory function, inadequate, 2
Restlessness, 1
Risk factors, number present, 83
Roles
   altered performance of, 7, 96
   change in, 41
   loss of significant, 48, 54
Room assignment, change in, 41, 48
Routine
   absence of, 29, 36
   change in established, 33, 60
Rudeness, 60

Sadness, 2, 8, 40, 41, 47
Scalp
   inability to scrub, 31
   scaling of, 31

Schedule conflicts, 60
Sedation, 83
Sedatives, 20, 36
Seizures, 63, 92
   potential for, 91
Self-care
   inability to provide, 41, 48, 54
   withdrawal from, 47
Self-care deficit, 1, 87
   bathing, 33–34, 96
   dressing, 24–26, 96
   eating, 27–28, 96
   feeding, 27, 96
   mobility, 19–23, 96
   personal hygiene, 31–32, 96
   toileting, 29–30, 96
Self-centered preoccupation, 40
Self-confidence, lack of, 20
Self-destructive behavior, 40, 53
Self-esteem
   disturbance in, 39
   lowered, 40, 47, 96
Self-feeding, slowness in, 66
Self-mutilation, 53
   risk for, 53, 96
Sensation, loss of, 29
Sensory deprivation, 2, 8, 41, 48, 54
Sensory overload, 2, 41, 48
Sensory/perceptual alterations, 1, 11, 15, 97
Separation from loved ones, 2, 41, 48, 54
Sequence, inability to, 31
Sexual behavior, inappropriate, 53
Sexual dysfunction, 97
Sexuality patterns, altered, 53, 97
Shaving, inability in, 31
Shoes
   impaired ability to tie, 24
   inability to clean/brush/polish, 31
Side vision, impaired, 11
Sighing, 47
Significant other, loss of, 54
Situational crisis, 54, 60
Skill deficit, 54
Skin breakdown, potential for, 83
Skin friction, 83
Skin integrity, impaired, 83, 91, 97
Skin-to-skin contact, 83
Sleep deprivation, 2
Sleeplessness, 48
Sleep pattern
   disturbance in, 1, 2, 97
   frequency in, 60
Slippery floors, 63
Smoking materials, carelessness with, 53
Snacking, 66
   excessive, 65
Soap, allergy to, 33
Social activities, decreased interest in, 2

Social graces, lack of, 60
Social interaction, impaired, 1, 7, 39, 47, 59, 97
Social isolation, 1, 39, 40, 47, 59, 66, 97
Socialization, alterations in, 59
Sociocultural dissonance, 60
Sore throat, 27
Speech
    disorganized, 1
    impaired, 36
    inabilities in, 15, 60
    inappropriate, 15
    incoherent, 1, 15
    slurred, 15
    whispered, 15
Sphincter control, loss of, 36
Spillage of foods/fluids, 31
Spiritual activities, decreased interest in, 2
Spiritual conflict, 54
Spiritual distress, 39, 40, 47, 97
Spiritual well-being, potential for enhanced, 39, 97
Splinting of joints, 20
Staff, conflict with, 40
Status change, 41
Stimuli, response to painful, 83
Stomach pain, 76
Strength
    decreased, 20, 29, 92
    impaired, 27, 33
Stress incontinence, 35
Suffocation, risk for, 97
Suicidal thoughts/actions, 47
Supplies, unavailability of needed, 31
Support structure, deterioration of, 80
Support system, lack of, 54
Surgery, recovering from, 20
Surgical trauma, 2
Swallowing
    difficulties in, 27, 66, 88
    impaired, 27, 71, 72, 87, 97
Syncope, 87, 88

Task
    inability to complete, 33
    unwillingness to perform, 31

Taste sensation, reported altered, 66
Tearfulness, 47
Teeth. See also Dental care
    carious, 72, 80
    improper brushing, 80
    loose, 72
    problems with, 79
Terminal illness, 54
Terminal prognosis, 8, 20, 60
Therapeutic diet, noncompliance with, 65
Therapeutic ineffectiveness, perceived, 54
Therapeutic regime
    management of, 96
    noncompliance with, 83
Thermoregulation, ineffective, 97
Thirst perception, 76
Thought processes
    altered, 1, 2, 7, 87, 97
    impaired, 60
Thyroid function, inadequate, 8
Time, disorientation to, 1, 7
Tissue integrity, impaired, 97
Tissue perfusion, altered, 87, 91, 97
Toileting, problems with, 29–30
Tongue, movements of, 16
Tranquilizing medications, 20
Transfer, inability to, 19, 29
Translocation syndrome, 60, 66
Trauma, 2, 11, 41, 48
    risk for, 97
Treatments
    frequent lengthy, 60
    resistance to, 92
Tremors, 87
Triggers, viii
Trunk/limb control, problems with, 20

Ulcers, 66
    decubitus, 83
    oral, 79
    pressure, 83–85
Unapproachability, 40
Underweight, 65
Uneven surfaces, 63
Unhappiness with nursing home placement, 41

Urinary elimination, 97
    altered, 35, 87
Urinary incontinence and indwelling catheter, 35–38
Urinary retention, 35, 87, 88, 97
Urinary tract infection, 35
Urine
    alkalinity of, 36
    collection of, 36
    excessive output of, 76

Value conflict, 54
Ventilation, inability to sustain spontaneous, 97
Verbally abusive behavior, 53
Verbal responses, inappropriate, 2, 7, 15
Violence, risk for self-directed or directed at others, 7, 47, 53, 87, 91, 97
Visual acuity, decreased, 20, 31
Visual deficit, 2, 11, 16, 41, 48, 63
Visual distortion/loss, 8
Visual field loss, 20
Visual function, 11–13
Vitamin B_{12} deficiency, 36
Vomiting, 27, 66, 76
Vulnerability, perceived, 54

Walking
    poor tolerance of, 19
    problems in, 19
    without assistance inappropriately, 63
Walkway, objects in, 63
Wandering, 53
Water temperature, inability to judge, 33
Weight gain, 65
Weight loss, 65, 71, 80
Wheelchair, inability to propel, 19
Withdrawal, 1, 87
Worrying, 53
Wound care therapeutic regime, noncompliance with, 91, 92
Wound drainage, 76
Wound healing, impaired, 91
Writing interventions, x